Hanna Hoof

Grammatiktraining Englisch dreifach differenziert

Kopiervorlagen für den Englischunterricht in der 5. Klasse

Die Autorin

Hanna Hoof ist studierte Realschullehrerin für die Fächer Englisch, Geschichte und Wirtschaft/Politik. Sie arbeitet an einer Gemeinschaftsschule in Schleswig-Holstein und sieht die Binnendifferenzierung in heterogenen Lerngruppen als ihren Arbeitsschwerpunkt.

2. Auflage 2022

AAP Lehrerwelt GmbH
Veritaskai 3
21079 Hamburg
Telefon: +49 (0) 40325083-040
E-Mail: info@lehrerwelt.de
Geschäftsführung: Christian Glaser
USt-ID: DE 173 77 61 42
Register: AG Hamburg HRB/126335

Wir verwenden in unseren Werken eine genderneutrale Sprache. Wenn keine neutrale Formulierung möglich ist, nennen wir die weibliche und die männliche Form. In Fällen, in denen wir aufgrund einer besseren Lesbarkeit nur ein Geschlecht nennen können, achten wir darauf, den unterschiedlichen Geschlechtsidentitäten gleichermaßen gerecht zu werden.

Autorschaft:	Hanna Hoof
Covergestaltung:	TSA&B Werbeagentur GmbH, Hamburg
Coverfoto:	© Africa Studio – stock.adobe.com
Illustrationen:	Ausrufezeichen (S. 9 u. a.) © Julia Flasche; alle weiteren Illustrationen © Christina Piper
Satz:	Typographie & Computer, Krefeld
Druck und Bindung:	SDK Systemdruck Köln GmbH & Co. KG, Köln

ISBN: 978-3-403-20364-3
www.persen.de

Inhaltsverzeichnis

Lehrerhinweise

Liebe Kolleginnen und Kollegen,

bei den vorliegenden Kopiervorlagen handelt es sich um dreifach differenziertes Unterrichtsmaterial zu den essenziellen Grammatikthemen in Klasse 5. Ihre Schülerinnen und Schüler erhalten die Möglichkeit, die bereits eingeführten Strukturen in Einzel- und Partnerarbeit zu üben und zu festigen. Mit dieser Materialsammlung können Sie ohne zeitaufwändige Recherche und Vorbereitung binnendifferenziert und dennoch gemeinsam mit allen Schülern arbeiten.

Aufbau:

Es gibt jede Kopiervorlage in drei Schwierigkeitsgraden. Die Unterschiede in den Anforderungsebenen sind durch Sterne gekennzeichnet: Ein Stern kennzeichnet das untere, zwei Sterne das mittlere und drei Sterne das obere Anforderungsniveau. Dabei wird der Inhalt weitestgehend beibehalten.
So wird bei allen drei Niveaus an den gleichen Aufgaben gearbeitet. Die Differenzierung findet meist durch die Variation der Hilfestellung, der Beispiele oder der Vorgaben statt. Dies ermöglicht eine unkomplizierte und gemeinsame Hinführung, Besprechung und Sicherung der Lösungen. Da die Aufgaben auf den verschiedenen Niveaus auf gleiche Weise aufgebaut sind, funktionieren die Partneraufgaben auch niveauübergreifend.

Die Kopiervorlagen sind in der Regel so konzipiert, dass sie mit zwei geschlossenen Aufgaben beginnen und mit einer offeneren Aufgabe schließen.

Veranschaulichung des Differenzierungsansatzes anhand von zwei Aufgaben:

Eine geschlossene Aufgabe zum Thema „adverbs of frequency“:

Niveau *

Setze die Wörter in den Klammern in die richtige Reihenfolge.

a. I ______________________________
(do – my homework – always) at the weekend.

Niveau * *

Put the words in the correct order.

a. do – at the weekend – my homework – I – always

____

Niveau * * *

Translate the German word in brackets into English und put the words in the right order.

a. do – the weekend – my homework – I – (immer) – at

Eine offene Partnerarbeit zum Thema „present progressive“:

Niveau *

Now you

a. Schreibe mithilfe des Kastens vier Fragen für deine(n) Sitznachbarin/Sitznachbarn in dein Heft. Lasse unter den Fragen Platz für eine Antwort.
b. Interviewe deine(n) Sitznachbarin/Sitznachbarn und notiere ihre/seine Antworten.

Lehrerhinweise

Am *Is* *Are*	your friend you ~~the sun~~ ~~our teacher~~ the classroom it your grandparents I your dog	wearing jeans? feeling good? working at the moment? raining outside? sitting on a chair? ~~shining today?~~ ~~reading something?~~ looking nice and tidy?

Examples: ***Is our teacher reading something?*** ***– No, he isn't. He's helping a student.***
Is the sun shining today? ***– Yes, it is.***

Niveau * *
Now you

a. Write down five questions in the present progressive for your partner in your exercise book. Leave some space for the answers. You can use the words from the box.
b. Interview your partner and write down the answers.

your friend you ~~the sun~~ ~~our teacher~~ the classroom it your grandparents I your dog	sit on a chair feel good work at the moment rain outside wear jeans ~~shine today~~ read something look nice and tidy

Examples:

Is our teacher reading something? ***– No, he isn't. He's helping a student.***

Is the sun shining today? ***– Yes, it is.***

Niveau * * *
Now you

a. Write down six questions in the present progressive for your partner in your exercise book. Leave some space for the answers.
b. Interview your partner and write down the answers.

Examples: ***Is your friend sitting on a chair?*** ***– Yes, he is.***
Is it raining today? ***– No, it isn't.***
Are your classmates sleeping? ***– ...***

Ich wünsche Ihren Schülern und Ihnen viel Freude und Erfolg bei der Arbeit mit dieser Materialsammlung.

Hanna Hoof

To be – positive and negative statements

1. Lisa's family

Vervollständige die Sätze mit den passenden Formen von „to be“. Beachte die Beispiele im Kasten.

I **am** ten years old.
You **are** from London.
Lindsay **is** nice.
We **are** a nice family.
You **are** a nice class.
The Webbers **are** in the kitchen.

a. Lisa __________ a girl from England.
b. I __________ in the car.
c. Bill __________ Lisa and Charly's father.
d. Michelle and Lindsay __________ funny.
e. Charly and Lisa, you __________ nice kids.
f. Charly, you __________ a funny boy!
g. I __________ in my bed.
h. We __________ the Webbers.

2. No, no, no!

Korrigiere die Aussagen. Benutze dabei die richtige Verneinung.

Examples: ***Charly is a girl.*** ***No, no, no! Charly isn't a girl. Charly is a boy.***
We are German. ***No, no, no! We aren't German. We are British.***

a. Lindsay is a horse.
No, no, no! Lindsay ______________ a horse. Lindsay __________ a cat.

b. Lisa and Charly are stupid.
No, no, no! Lisa and Charly ______________ stupid. Lisa and Charly __________ clever.

c. I am from New York.
No, no, no! You ______________ from New York. You __________ from Manchester.

d. Mr. Marty, you are a student.
No, no, no! I ______________ a student. I __________ a teacher.

3. About you

Schreibe vier Sätze über deine Familie, deine Haustiere und dich. Benutze die Wörter aus Box 1 und Box 2.

Box 1	***Example:***			**Box 2**
My dog	*My dog*	*isn't*	*stupid.*	pretty
My hamster		is		brown
My mother		isn't		young
My father		are		nice
My sister		'm not		sweet
My brother		aren't		stupid
My parents		am		... years old
I				clever
				old

To be – positive and negative statements

*** ***

1. Lisa's family

Complete the sentences with the correct forms of 'to be':
am – **is** – **are**.

Example: ***Charly ___is___ six years old.***

a. Lisa ________ a girl from England.

b. I ________ in the car.

c. Bill ________ Lisa and Charly's father.

d. Michelle and Lindsay ________ funny.

e. Charly and Lisa, you ________ nice kids.

f. Charly, you ________ a funny boy!

g. I ________ in my bed.

h. We ________ the Webbers.

2. No, no, no!

Correct the statements. Look at the example.

Example: ***Charly is a girl.*** ***No, no, no! Charly isn't a girl. Charly is a boy.***

a. Lindsay is a horse.

No, no, no! Lindsay ____________________. ____________________ a cat.

b. Lisa and Charly are stupid.

No, no, no! Lisa and Charly ____________________. ____________________ clever.

c. I am from New York.

No, no, no! You ____________________. ____________________ from Manchester.

d. Mr. Marty, you are a student.

No, no, no! I ____________________. ____________________ a teacher.

3. About you

Write five sentences about your family and your pets in your exercise book. You can use the words from the boxes.

Example: ***My dog isn't stupid.***

My dog My hamster My mother My father My sister My brother My parents I We	isn't are is 'm not aren't am	pretty brown young nice sweet stupid ... years old clever old

To be – positive and negative statements

***

1. Lisa's family

Complete the sentences with the correct forms of 'to be'.

Example: ***Charly ___is___ six years old.***

a. Lisa __________ a girl from England.

b. I __________ in the car.

c. Bill __________ Lisa and Charly's father.

d. Michelle and Lindsay __________ funny.

e. Charly and Lisa, you __________ nice kids.

f. Charly, you __________ a funny boy!

g. I __________ in my bed.

h. We __________ the Webbers.

2. No, no, no!

First complete the sentences. Then correct the statements. Look at the example.

Example: ***Charly is a girl.*** ***No, no, no! Charly isn't a girl. Charly is a boy.***

a. Lindsay ________ a horse.

No, no, no! Lindsay ____________________. ____________________ a cat.

b. Lisa and Charly ________ stupid.

No, no, no! Lisa and Charly ____________________. ____________________ clever.

c. I ________ from New York.

No, no, no! You ____________________. ____________________ from Manchester.

d. Mr. Marty, you ________ a student.

No, no, no! I ____________________. ____________________ a teacher.

3. About you

Write six sentences about your family and your pets in your exercise book. Use the words from the box.

Examples: ***My dog isn't stupid.***
My father is clever.

aren't	is	'm not	clever	brown	nice	old	sweet
are	am	isn't	stupid	pretty	young	from ...	

To be (short forms) and personal pronouns

*

1. Hello, we're the Webbers!

Trage die passenden Personalpronomen aus dem Kasten in die Lücken ein.

Es werden nicht alle Personalpronomen benötigt.

I	you	he	she	it	we	you	they

a. This is my car. ***It*** 's blue.

b. Hey kids, ______'re too loud! Shhhh!

c. I'm Lisa and this is my brother Charly. ______ live in Birdhurst Road.

d. _____'m the sweet cat Lindsay. Meeeooow!

e. This is Bill. ______'s Lisa's dad.

f. The Webbers are from London. ______ speak English.

2. He's in the garden.

Ersetze die Langformen durch die passenden Kurzformen. Beachte den Kasten.

Langform		Kurzform
I am	➡	I'm
you are	➡	you're
he is / she is / it is	➡	he's / she's / it's
we are	➡	we're
you are	➡	you're
they are	➡	they're

a. It is a nice day. ➡ ____________________

b. I am from Germany. ➡ ____________________

c. They are from London. ➡ ____________________

d. We are in the classroom. ➡ ____________________

3. Wow! It's a yellow cat!

Trage die passenden Kurzformen aus dem Kasten in die Lücken ein.

you're	we're	it's	~~I'm~~	they're	she's

a. How old are you? – ***I'm*** ten.

b. Where are the kids? – ________ at school.

c. Where's Lisa? – ________ in the classroom.

d. Look at this dog! ________ a sweet dog.

e. It's ten o'clock! ________ late, boys!

f. Hey girls, how are you? – ________ fine, thanks.

4. We're funny.

Schreibe mit den Wörtern aus dem Kasten vier Sätze in dein Heft.

I you she you we they	're 's 'm	smart pretty from Germany silly in the classroom late

Example: ***She's from Germany.***

To be (short forms) and personal pronouns

1. Hello, we're the Webbers!
Fill in the gaps with the correct personal pronouns from the box.

I	you	he	she	~~it~~	we	you	they

a. This is my car. ________'s blue.

b. Hey kids, ________'re too loud! Shhhh!

c. I'm Lisa and this is my brother Charly. ________ live in Birdhurst Road.

d. _____'m the sweet cat Lindsay. Meeeooow!

e. This is Bill. ________'s Lisa's dad.

f. The Webbers are from London. ________ speak English.

g. Hey Charly, how old are ________?

h. This is Lisa. ________'s a nice girl.

2. He's in the garden.
Write sentences with the correct short forms from the box.

Short forms
I'm you're he's / she's / it's we're you're they're

a. It is a nice day. ➡ ______________________________

b. I am from Germany. ➡ ______________________________

c. They are from London. ➡ ______________________________

d. We are in the classroom. ➡ ______________________________

3. Wow! It's a yellow cat!
Fill in the gaps with the correct short forms.

a. How old are you? – ***I'm*** ten.

b. Where are the kids? – ________ at school.

c. Where's Lisa? – ________ in the classroom

d. Look at this dog! ________ a sweet dog.

e. It's ten o'clock! ________ late, boys!

f. Hey girls, how are you? – ________ fine, thanks.

g. What's your phone number? – ________ 04932.

h. I love you! ________ so nice and pretty.

4. We're funny.
Write five sentences in your exercise book. Use the words from the box.

it I you she we they he	(be)	in the kitchen smart pretty from Germany in the classroom late silly

Example: ***She's from Germany.***

To be (short forms) and personal pronouns ***

1. Hello, we're the Webbers!

Fill in the gaps with the correct personal pronouns.

***Example:* Where is the green book? – __It's__ on the table.**

a. This is my car. ________'s blue.

b. Hey kids, ________'re too loud! Shhhh!

c. I'm Lisa and this is my brother Charly. ________live in Birdhurst Road.

d. _____'m the sweet cat Lindsay. Meeeooow!

e. This is Bill. ________'s Lisa's dad.

f. The Webbers are from London. ________ speak English.

g. Hey Charly, how old are ________?

h. This is Lisa. ________'s a nice girl.

2. He's in the garden.

Write sentences with the correct short forms.

***Example:* You are a nice teacher. ➡ You're a nice teacher.**

a. It is a nice day. ➡ ____________________

b. I am from Germany. ➡ ____________________

c. They are from London. ➡ ____________________

d. We are in the classroom. ➡ ____________________

3. Wow! It's a yellow cat!

Fill in the gaps with the correct short forms.

a. How old are you? – ***__I'm__*** ten.

b. Where are the kids? – ________ at school.

c. Where's Lisa? – ________ in the classroom

d. Look at this dog! ________ a sweet dog.

e. It's ten o'clock! ________ late, boys!

f. Hey girls, how are you? – ________ fine, thanks.

g. What's your phone number? – ________ 04932.

h. I love you! ________ so nice and pretty.

i. That's Mr. Marty. ________ a nice teacher.

j. Where is my ball? – ________ in the bag.

4. We're funny.

Write seven sentences in your exercise book.
Use the words from box 1 and from box 2.

Box 1	
it I you she we they he	(be)

Box 2	
clever on the table in the shop at work on the sofa	in the classroom late funny a funny dad a nice family

***Example:* You're a happy girl.**

To be – questions

*

1. Is Lisa a crazy girl?

Ordne den Fragen die richtigen Antworten zu, indem du Linien ziehst.

a. Is Lisa a crazy girl?	1. No, we aren't.
b. Are we from Denmark, Mum?	2. Yes, you are, Lisa.
c. Are the Webbers from Germany?	3. Yes, she is.
d. Hey Charly, am I your favourite sister?	4. No, they aren't.

2. Is green your favourite colour?

Sortiere die Wörter so, dass du die richtigen Fragen zu den vorgegebenen Antworten erhälst.

Example: ***sweet – chocolate – is***

Is chocolate sweet? ______ ***Yes, it is.***

a. your mother – from Berlin – is

______ Yes, she is.

b. blue – is – your favourite colour

______ No, it isn't.

c. are – pink – elephants

______ No, they aren't.

d. I – am – pretty

______ Yes, you are.

e. your schoolbag – green – is

______ No, it isn't.

3. How are you?

a. Verbinde die Wörter zu sinnvollen Fragen, indem du Linien ziehst. Beachte das Beispiel.
b. Beantworte die Fragen in ganzen Sätzen. Auch hier hilft dir das Beispiel.

a.		**b.**
a. ***Where***	1. name?	1. ***It's under my desk.***
b. How old	2. ***is your schoolbag?***	2. ______
c. Who's	3. you?	3. ______
d. How are	4. are you?	4. ______
e. What's your	5. your English teacher?	5. ______

To be – questions

*** ***

1. Is Lisa a crazy girl?

a. Fill in the gaps. Use the correct form of 'to be': **am – is – are**
b. Match the questions and the answers. Draw lines.

a. _______ Lisa a crazy girl?	1. No, we aren't.
b. _______ we from Denmark, Mum?	2. Yes, you are, Lisa.
c. _______ the Webbers from Germany?	3. Yes, she is.
d. Hey Charly, _______ I your favourite sister?	4. No, they aren't.

2. Is green your favourite colour?

Put the words in the correct order to get the questions to the answers.

Example:* *sweet – chocolate – is	*it – is – yes*
Is chocolate sweet?	***Yes, it is.***
a. your mother – from Berlin – is	yes – is – she
____________________	____________
b. blue – is – your favourite colour	isn't – no – it
____________________	____________
c. are – pink – elephants	no – aren't – they
____________________	____________
d. I – am – pretty	are – yes – you
____________________	____________
e. your schoolbag – green – is	no – isn't – it
____________________	____________

3. How are you?

a. Match the two parts of the sentences to get the right questions. Draw lines.
b. Answer the questions in full sentences. Look at the example .

a.		**b.**
a. Where	1. name?	1. ***It's under my desk.***
b. How old	2. is your schoolbag?	2. ____________
c. Who's	3. you?	3. ____________
d. How are	4. are you?	4. ____________
e. What's your	5. your English teacher?	5. ____________

To be – questions

* * *

1. Is Lisa a crazy girl?
a. Fill in the gaps. Use the correct form of 'to be'.
b. Match the questions and the answers by drawing lines. Then complete the answers.

a. ______ Lisa a crazy girl?	1. No, we ______.
b. ______ we from Denmark, Mum?	2. Yes, you ______, Lisa.
c. ______ the Webbers from Germany?	3. Yes, she ______.
d. Hey Charly, ______ I your favourite sister?	4. No, they ______.

2. Is green your favourite colour?
Make questions and answers. Put the words in the correct order.

Example: *it – ? – is – sweet – yes – chocolate – is*

Is chocolate sweet? – Yes, it is.

a. is – from Berlin– yes – she – ? – is – your mother

____

b. blue – isn't – ? – your favourite colour – it – is – no

____

c. they – elephants – aren't – are – pink – no – ?

____

d. pretty – yes – I – ? – are – you – am

____

e. your schoolbag – ? – it – is – no – isn't – green

____

3. How are you?
a. Match the two parts of the sentences to get the right questions. Draw lines.
b. Answer the questions in full sentences. Look at the example.
c. Think of two questions with question words for 6 and 7 and answer the questions.

a.		**b.**
a. Where	1. name?	1. ***It's under my desk.***
b. How old	2. is your schoolbag?	2. ______
c. Who's	3. you?	3. ______
d. How are	4. are you?	4. ______
e. What's your	5. your English teacher?	5. ______
c. ______________________ ?		6. ______
______________________ ?		7. ______

Can

*****

1. Can they do it?

Trage **can** oder **can't** ein.

Example: ***Yes, I __can__ ride a horse!***

a. No, Lindsay ________ read a book! It's a cat!

b. Yes, Charly and Lisa ________ play football. They're really good!

c. Where are you, Bill? I ________ see you.

d. Mmmhhh! Yummy! Michelle, you ________ cook!

e. Yes, Mr. Marty ________ play the guitar! He's the music teacher.

2. About you

Beantworte die Fragen mit Kurzformen wie in den Beispielen.

Examples: ***Can you spell your name?*** – ***Yes, I can.***

Can you throw a ball to the moon? – ***No, I can't.***

a. Can you sing? – ________________

b. Can your mother play tennis? – ________________

c. Can your friend climb a tree? – ________________

d. Can your father cook spaghetti? – ________________

3. Yes, we can play football!

Schaue dir die Antworten an und stelle dazu die passenden Fragen. Beachte das Beispiel.

Example: ***Can you swim?*** ***– No, I can't swim.***

a. ____________________________? – Yes, birds can fly.

b. ____________________________? – No, we can't watch TV now.

c. ____________________________? – Yes, you can go home.

d. ____________________________? – No, they can't buy a new car.

4. Interview your partner

a. Schreibe vier Interviewfragen mithilfe der Wörter aus dem Kasten in dein Heft. Lasse hinter jeder Frage Platz für eine Antwort.

b. Interviewe deine(n) Sitznachbarin/Sitznachbarn und schreibe ihre/seine Antworten auf.

Examples: ***Can a parrot read the newspaper? – No, it can't.***

Can you fly to the moon? – Yes, I can.

Can	you the President of America your hamster Santa Claus your parents your PE teacher a parrot	fly to the moon ride a bike read the newspaper play the piano rap make good pancakes ride a horse	?

Can

*** ***

1. Can they do it?
Fill in the gaps with 'can' or 'can't' and the verb.

Example: ***Yes, I __can ride__ (ride) a horse!***

a. No, Lindsay ____________ (read) a book! It's a cat!
b. Yes, Charly and Lisa __________ (play) football. They're really good!
c. Where are you, Bill? I ____________ (see) you.
d. Mmmhhh! Yummy! Michelle, you ____________ (cook)!
e. Yes, Mr. Marty ____________ (play) the guitar! He's the music teacher.

2. About you
Put the words in the correct order to make questions with 'can'. Then answer the questions with short answers.

Example: ***you – your name – can – spell***
Can you spell your name? – ***Yes, I can. / No, I can't.***

a. you – sing – can
____________________________________? – ____________________

b. play tennis – can – your mother
____________________________________? – ____________________

c. your friend – can – climb a tree
____________________________________? – ____________________

d. cook spaghetti – can – your father
____________________________________? – ____________________

3. Yes, we can play football!
a. Look at the sentences on the right. Fill in 'can' or 'can't'.
b. Now look at the sentences again and write down the correct questions on the left.

Example: ***Can you swim?*** ***– No, I can't swim.***

a. ____________________________________? – Yes, birds ______ fly.
b. ____________________________________? – No, we ______ watch TV now.
c. ____________________________________? – Yes, you ______ go home.
d. ____________________________________? – No, they ______ buy a new car.

4. Interview your partner
a. Write down five interview questions with 'can' for your partner. Leave space for the answers.
b. Interview your partner and write down her/his answers. You can use the words from the box or other words.

Example: ***Can you make good pancakes? – Yes, I can.***

dance **play the piano** **sing** **swim** **jump high** **tell a joke** **rap** **ride a horse**

Can

1. Can they do it?
Fill in the gaps with the correct form of 'can' and the verb.

a. No, Lindsay ________ (read) a book! It's a cat!
b. Yes, Charly and Lisa ________ (play) football. They're really good!
c. Where are you, Bill? I ________ (see) you.
d. Mmmhhh! Yummy! Michelle, you ________ (cook)!
e. Yes, Mr. Marty ________ (play) the guitar! He's the music teacher.
f. Yes, I ________ (ride) a horse.

2. About you
Put the words in the correct order to make questions with 'can'. Then answer the questions with short answers.

a. you – sing – can
________________________________? – ________________
b. play tennis – can – your mother
________________________________? – ________________
c. your friend – can – climb a tree
________________________________? – ________________
d. cook spaghetti – can – your father
________________________________? – ________________
e. your music teacher – play – can – the piano
________________________________? – ________________

3. Yes, we can play football!
a. Look at the answers on the right. Fill in 'can' or 'can't' + verb.
b. Now look at the answers again and write down the correct questions on the left.

Example: ***Can you swim?*** ***– No, I can't swim (swim).***

a. ________________________________? – Yes, birds ________ (fly).
b. ________________________________? – No, we ________ (watch TV) now.
c. ________________________________? – Yes, you ________ (go) home.
d. ________________________________? – No, they ________ (buy) a new car.
e. ________________________________? – Yes, my sister ________(jump) high.

4. Interview your partner
a. Write down six interview questions with 'can' for your partner. Leave space for the answers.
b. Interview your partner and write down his answers.

Example: ***Can you sing Jingle Bells? – Yes, I can.***

Have got

1. What have they got?

Schaue dir die Bilder an und vervollständige dann mit **have got** oder **has got** den Text.

Example: ***Picture 1: We have got a bike.***

Picture 2: It ____________________ a fish.

Picture 3: I ____________________ a ball.

Picture 4: You ____________________ a book.

Picture 5: They ____________________ a laptop.

2. What they haven't got …

Schreibe nun mithilfe der Bilder auf, was die Webbers nicht haben. Verwende **haven't got** oder **hasn't got**.

Example: ***Picture 1: We haven't got a fish, a ball, a book or a laptop.***

Picture 2: It ___________ a bike, a ball, a book or a laptop.

Picture 3: I ___________ a bike, a fish, a book or a laptop.

Picture 4: You ___________ a bike, a fish, a ball or a laptop.

Picture 5: They ___________ a bike, a fish, a ball or a book.

3. Have you got a ball?

Vervollständige die Fragen wie in den Beispielen.

Examples: ***Has Lisa got a ball? – Yes, she has.***
Have you got a fish, Charly? – No, I haven't.

a. _________ Charly got a bike? – No, he __________________.

b. _________ you got a fish, Lindsay? – Yes, I __________________.

c. _________ Lisa and Charly got a laptop? – Yes, they __________________.

d. Michelle and Bill, _________ you got a fish? – No, we __________________.

4. Has your mum got a pink bed?

a. Schreibe vier Fragen für deine(n) Sitznachbarin / Sitznachbarn in dein Heft. Lass unter jeder Frage eine Zeile frei. Benutze die Wörter aus dem Kasten.

Have **Has**	you **your grandmother** your boyfriend	your brother your teacher your friend	**got**	a pink car **funny hair** yellow eyes	silly friends a girlfriend white teeth	**?**

b. Interviewe nun deine(n) Sitznachbarin/Sitznachbarn und schreibe die Antworten auf.

Example: ***Has your grandmother got funny hair? – Yes, she has.***

Have got

*** ***

1. What have they got?
Look at the pictures and fill in in the gaps with 'have got' or 'has got'.

1 Michelle and Bill	2 The cat Lindsay	3 Lisa	4 Charly	5 Lisa and Charly

Picture 1: We __________ a bike.
Picture 2: It __________ a fish.
Picture 3: I __________ a ball.
Picture 4: You __________ a book.
Picture 5: They __________ a laptop.

2. What they haven't got ...
Take another look at the pictures and write down what the Webbers **haven't got**. Use 'hasn't got' or 'haven't got'.

Example: ***Picture 1: We haven't got a fish, a ball, a book or a laptop.***

Picture 2: It __________ a bike, a ball, a book or a laptop.
Picture 3: I __________ a bike, a fish, a book or a laptop.
Picture 4: You __________ a bike, a fish, a ball or a laptop.
Picture 5: They __________ a bike, a fish, a ball or a book.

3. Have you got a ball?
Complete the questions and answers for the Webbers. Use the pictures.

Example: ***Lindsay, have you got a laptop? – No, I haven't.***

a. ________ Charly ________ a bike? – No, he __________.
b. ________ you ________ a fish, Lindsay? – Yes, I __________.
c. ________ Lisa and Charly ________ a laptop? – Yes,they __________.
d. Michelle and Bill, ________ you ________ a fish? – No, we __________.

4. Has your mum got a pink bed?
a. Write down five questions for your partner in your exercise book. You can use the words from the box or other words. Leave space for the answers.
b. Interview your partner. Write down her/his answers.

white teeth   green hair   you   your hamster   your sister   your parents funny hair   your teacher   your girlfriend   silly friends   a pretty smile   a black car

Examples: ***Has your grandmother got a pretty smile? – Yes, she has.***
Have you got a big room? – No, I ...

Have got

1. What have they got?

Look at the pictures and finish the sentences.

1 Michelle and Bill	2 The cat Lindsay	3 Lisa	4 Charly	5 Lisa and Charly

Picture 1: We ________________________.

Picture 2: It ________________________.

Picture 3: I ________________________.

Picture 4: You ________________________.

Picture 5: They ________________________.

2. What they haven't got ...

Take another look at the pictures and write down what the Webbers **haven't got**.

Example: Picture 1: We haven't got a fish, a ball, a book or a laptop.

Picture 2: It ____.

Picture 3: I ____.

Picture 4: You ____.

Picture 5: They ____.

3. Have you got a ball?

Complete the questions and answers for the Webbers. Use the pictures.

Example: Lindsay, have you got a laptop? – No, I haven't.

a. ________ Charly ________ a bike? – ***No, he ...*** ________________________.

b. ________ you ____________ a fish, Lindsay? – ________________________.

c. ________ Lisa and Charly ________ a laptop? – ________________________.

d. Michelle and Bill, ________ you ________ a fish? – ________________________.

4. Has your mum got a pink bed?

a. Write down ten six questions for your partner in your exercise book. Leave space for the answers.

b. Interview your partner. Write down her/his answers.

Examples: Has your brother got a pretty smile? – No, he hasn't.
Have you got a big room? – Yes, I ...

The s-genitive and the possessive determiners

*

1. The hamster's hut is pink

Setze die richtige Form des s-Genitivs in die Lücken ein: **'s** oder **s'**.

In eine Lücke musst du gar nichts eintragen.

Examples: ***The Webbers' house is in London.*** ***Lisa's brother is …***

a. The teacher____ name is Marty.

b. Charly____ bed is big and blue.

c. Lisa____ and Charly____ parents are outside.

d. The kids____ pool is over there. Look!

e. My sister____ room isn't big.

f. The Johnsons____ house is across the street.

2. Your eyes are pretty!

Wähle die passenden Possessivbegleiter aus und trage sie in die Lücken ein.

a. Oh no! I can't find ______ (his / my) mobile phone!

b. Wow! Bill, ______ (your / its) shirt is nice.

c. The Webbers love ______ (her / their) big garden.

d. Michelle has got a tomato on ______ (her / his) sandwich.

e. Charly hasn't got a chair in ______ (my / his) room.

f. Oh no! We can't find ______ (its / our) cat Lindsay!

g. Kids! Hurry up! Where are ______ (your / their) shoes?

h. The hamster Donald is in ______ (his / my) cage.

3. Is your teacher's hair grey?

Beantworte die Fragen. Benutze dabei die richtigen Possessivbegleiter:
my, its, his, her, your, their or **our**

Examples: ***Is your house big?*** ***– No, my / our house isn't big.***
Is your uncle's car red? ***– Yes, his car is red.***

a. Is your mother's bed small? – No, ______________________________.

b. Is your father's phone new? – Yes, ______________________________.

c. Is your parents' garden nice? – No, ______________________________.

d. Is an elephant's head big? – Yes, ______________________________.

e. Is your teacher's hair grey? – No, ______________________________.

4. Now you

Überlege dir mithilfe des Kastens drei Fragen für deine(n) Sitznachbarin/Sitznachbarn mit der richtigen Form des s-Genitivs und schreibe sie in dein Heft. Führe das Interview durch und notiere die Antworten.

Example: ***Are your teacher's eyes blue? – No, they aren't. His eyes are brown.***

Is Are	your father your friend your parents ~~teacher's~~	+ s-Genitiv	~~eyes blue~~ car green house big feet small	?

The s-genitive and the possessive determiners

1. The hamster's hut is pink

Fill in the gaps with the correct s-genitive.

In one gap there is nothing to fill in.

Examples: ***The Webbers' house is in London.*** ***Lisa's brother is …***

a. The teacher____ name is Marty.
b. Charly____ bed is big and blue.
c. Lisa____ and Charly____ parents are outside.
d. The kids____ pool is over there. Look!
e. My sister____ room isn't big.
f. The Johnsons____ house is across the street.
g. Is this Bill____ car? – No, it's Thomas____ car.
h. I'm sure, that Batman is Superman____ friend.

2. Your eyes are pretty!

Fill in the correct possessive determiners from the box.

his (2x)	**my**	**their**	**her**	**your (2x)**	**our**

a. Oh no! I can't find ______ mobile phone!
b. Wow! Bill, ______ shirt is nice.
c. The Webbers love ______ big garden.
d. Michelle has got a tomato on ______ sandwich.
e. Charly hasn't got a chair in ______ room.
f. Oh no! We can't find ______ cat Lindsay!
g. Kids! Hurry up! Where are ______ shoes?
h. The hamster Donald is in ______ cage.

3. Is your teacher's hair grey?

Answer the questions and use the correct possessive determiners:
my, its, his, her, your, their or **our**

Examples: ***Is your house big?*** ***– No, my/our house isn't big.***
Is your uncle's car red? ***– Yes, his car is red.***

a. Is your mother's bed small? – No, ______________________________.
b. Is your father's phone new? – Yes, ______________________________.
c. Is your parents' garden nice? – No, ______________________________.
d. Is an elephant's head big? – Yes, ______________________________.
e. Is your teacher's hair grey? – No, ______________________________.
f. Is your classroom pretty? – Yes, ______________________________.
g. Are your friends' bikes cool? – No, ______________________________.

4. Now you

Think of three questions with the s-genitive for your partner and write them in your exercise book. Interview your partner and write down the answers.

Examples: ***Is your mother's hair red? – No, it isn't. Her hair is brown.***
Is your parents' car black? – Yes, …

The s-genitive and the possessive determiners

1. The hamster's hut is pink

Fill in the gaps with the correct s-genitive.

In one gap there is nothing to fill in.

***Example:* Lisa'<u>s</u> brother is in the garden.**

a. The teacher____ name is Marty.

b. Charly____ bed is big and blue.

c. Lisa____ and Charly____ parents are outside.

d. The kids____ pool is over there. Look!

e. My sister____ room isn't big.

f. The Johnsons____ house is across the street.

g. Is this Bill____ car? – No, it's Thomas____ car.

h. I'm sure, that Batman is Superman____ friend.

i. The Webbers____ house is in London.

j. The students____ cafeteria is over there!

2. Your eyes are pretty!

Fill in the correct possessive determiners.

***Examples:* They have got two bathrooms in <u>their</u> house.**
I want to have a big chocolate cake on <u>my</u> birthday.

a. Oh no! I can't find ______ mobile phone!

b. Wow! Bill, ______ shirt is nice.

c. The Webbers love ______ big garden.

d. Michelle has got a tomato on ______ sandwich.

e. Charly hasn't got a chair in ______ room.

f. Oh no! We can't find ______ cat Lindsay!

g. Kids! Hurry up! Where are ______ shoes?

h. The hamster Donald is in ______ cage.

3. Is your teacher's hair grey?

Answer the questions and use the correct possessive determiners:

***Examples:* Is <u>your</u> house big? – No, <u>my / our</u> house isn't big. It is small.**
Is your uncle'<u>s</u> car red? – Yes, <u>his</u> car is red.

a. Is your mother's bed small? – No, ______________________________.

b. Is your father's phone new? – Yes, ______________________________.

c. Is your parents' garden nice? – No, ______________________________.

d. Is an elephant's head big? – Yes, ______________________________.

e. Is your teacher's hair grey? – No, ______________________________.

f. Is your classroom pretty? – Yes, ______________________________.

g. Are your friends' bikes cool? – No, ______________________________.

4. Now you

Think of three questions with the s-genitive for your partner and write them in your exercise book. Interview your partner and write down the answers.

***Example:* Is your mother's hair red? – No, it isn't. Her hair is brown.**

The simple present – positive statements

1. Lisa's Monday

Trage die richtigen Verbformen in die Lücken ein.

He, she, it – das *s* muss mit!

On Mondays Lisa ***gets up*** (get up) at 7 o'clock. She ____________ (like) breakfast and ____________ (eat) a sandwich before she ____________ (go) to school. "I ____________ (love) sandwiches," she always ____________ (say) to her mum. In the school bus she ____________ (sit) next to a nice boy. His name is Alex and he often ____________ (smile) at Lisa. Lisa and Alex only sometimes ____________ (talk), but they always ____________ (say) "Hi!" and "Bye". At school the teacher ____________ (ask) the children about the weekend every Monday. In the classroom Lisa ____________ (think) about Alex from the bus.

2. You eat my pizza every Saturday!

Bringe die Wörter in die richtige Reihenfolge.

Example: ***my horse – kiss – I – every*** ➡ ***I kiss my horse every day.***

a. you – coffee – drink – every Sunday

____

b. Charly – football – every week – plays

____

c. Alex – every morning – Lisa – meets

____

3. My weekend

Schreibe vier Sätze über dein Wochenende in dein Heft.
Du kannst die Wörter aus dem Kasten verwenden.

Example: ***On Friday afternoon I do my English homework.***

On Friday afternoon I ... On Saturday morning I ... On Saturday afternoon I ... On Saturday night I ... On Sunday I ...	play football read a book do the homework relax play with my cat / dog chat with my friends	play on the PC do my English homework watch TV help my dad in the kitchen sleep in my bed talk to the flowers in my garden

The simple present – positive statements

1. Lisa's Monday

Fill in the gaps with the correct verb forms.

On Mondays Lisa ***gets up*** (get up) at 7 o'clock. She ______________ (like) breakfast and ______________ (eat) a sandwich before she ______________ (go) to school. "I ______________ (love) sandwiches," she always ______________ (say) to her mum. In the school bus she ______________ (sit) next to a nice boy. His name is Alex and he often ______________ (smile) at Lisa. Lisa and Alex only sometimes ______________ (talk), but they always ______________ (say) "Hi!" and "Bye". At school the teacher ______________ (ask) the children about the weekend every Monday. In the classroom Lisa ______________ (think) about Alex from the bus. Sometimes the teacher ______________ (say), "Lisa, you never ______________ (listen)! Come on! Say something about your weekend." Lisa answers, "My weekends ______________ (be) boring. I ______________ (be) always happy when it's Monday."

2. You eat my pizza every Saturday!

Bring the words in the correct order. Then circle the correct verb form and write down the sentence.

Example: ***my horse – kiss/kisses – I – every day*** ➡ ***I kiss my horse every day.***

a. you – coffee – drink/drinks – every Sunday

____

b. Charly – football – every week – play/plays

____

c. Alex – every morning – Lisa – meet/meets

____

3. My weekend

Write five sentences about your weekend in your exercise book. You can use the words from the box.

Example: ***On Friday afternoon I do my English homework.***

play football	play on the PC
tidy up my room	watch TV
do the homework	help my dad in the kitchen
play with my cat/dog	sleep in my bed
chat with my friends	talk to the flowers in my garden

The simple present – positive statements

1. Lisa's Monday

Fill in the gaps with the correct verb forms.

On Mondays Lisa ______________ (get up) at 7 o'clock. She ______________ (like) break-fast and ______________ (eat) a sandwich before she ______________ (go) to school. "I ______________ (love) sandwiches," she always ______________ (say) to her mum. In the school bus she ______________ (sit) next to a nice boy. His name is Alex and he often ______________ (smile) at Lisa. Lisa and Alex only sometimes ______________ (talk), but they always ______________ (say) "Hi!" and "Bye". At school the teacher ______________ (ask) the children about the weekend every Monday. In the class-room Lisa ______________ (think) about Alex from the bus. Sometimes the teacher ______________ (say), "Lisa, you never ______________ (listen)! Come on! Say something about your weekend." Lisa answers, "My weekends ______________ (be) boring. I ______________ (be) always happy when it's Monday." Her friend Ann always ______________ (laugh) and ______________ (say): "You ______________ (think) about Alex every day!"

2. You eat my pizza every Saturday!

Bring the words in the correct order. Then circle the correct verb form and write down the sentence.

a. my horse – kiss / kisses – I – every day

____

b. you – coffee – drink / drinks – every Sunday

____

c. Charly – football – every week – play / plays

____

d. Alex – every morning – Lisa – meet / meets

____

e. Michelle – every afternoon – the newspaper – read / reads

____

3. My weekend

Write six sentences about your weekend in your exercise book. You can use the words from the box.

Example:* *On Friday afternoon I do my English homework.

play football	play on the PC
tidy up my room	watch TV
do the homework	help my dad in the kitchen
play with my cat / dog	sleep in my bed
chat with my friends	talk to the flowers in my garden

The simple present – negative statements

*

1. We don't like smelly cheese!
Trage **don't** oder **doesn't** in die Lücken ein.

a. I ____________ like pizza. Hamburgers are much better.

b. Charly and Bill ____________ play tennis every Sunday. They watch football.

c. No, Lisa! ____________ watch TV now! Do your homework, please.

d. Michelle ____________ go shopping in London. It's too noisy.

e. No, we ____________ play on the PC every day. It's boring.

2. It's all wrong!
Berichtige die Sätze wie im Beispiel. Ergänze dazu **doesn't / don't** und das Vollverb.

Example: ***Lisa loves her hamster John. – No! Lisa doesn't love her hamster John. She loves her cat Lindsay.***

a. Rabbits eat steak. – No! Rabbits ______________________ steak. They eat carrots.

b. You drink beer every morning. – No! I ______________________ beer every morning. I drink coffee.

c. I love chocolate for breakfast. – No! You ______________________ chocolate for breakfast. You love sandwiches.

d. We go ice skating in summer. – No! We ______________________ ice skating in summer. We go ice skating in winter.

e. Alex reads a book every night. – No! Alex ______________________ a book every night. He watches TV.

3. About you and your family
Was mag deine Familie nicht? Schreibe mindestens fünf Sätze in dein Heft.
Du kannst die Wörter aus dem Kasten verwenden.

Example: ***My sister doesn't like fish.***

My mother My parents I My brother / sister My cousins My grandmother My grandfather My uncle My aunt We My father	**doesn't like / don't like**	cats fish Mondays cheese rats tattoos boys noisy children bananas pink hair piercings

The simple present – negative statements 

1. We don't like smelly cheese!
Fill in 'don't' or 'doesn't' and the verb.

Example: ***Ugh! We don't like (like) smelly cheese.***

a. I ______________________ (like) pizza. Hamburgers are much better.
b. Charly and Bill ______________________ (play) tennis every Sunday. They watch football.
c. No, Lisa! ______________________ (watch) TV now! Do your homework, please.
d. Michelle ______________________ (go) shopping in London. It's too noisy.
e. No, we ______________________ (play) on the PC every day. It's boring.

2. It's all wrong!
Correct the sentences.

Example: ***Lisa loves her hamster John. (cat Lindsay)***
No! Lisa doesn't love her hamster John. She loves her cat Lindsay.

a. Rabbits eat steak. (carrots) – ***No! Rabbits*** ______________________
____.
b. You drink beer every morning. (coffee) – No! I ______________________
____.
c. I love chocolate for breakfast. (sandwiches) – No! You ______________________
____.
d. We go ice skating in summer. (winter) – No! We ______________________
____.
e. Alex reads a book every night. (watch TV) – No! Alex ______________________
____.

3. About you and your family
Write six sentences about what your family doesn't like in your exercise book.
You can use the words from the box or other words.

Example: ***My grandfather doesn't like tattoos.***

My mother My parents I My brother / sister My cousins My grandmother My grandfather My uncle My aunt We My father	**not / like**	cats fish Mondays cheese rats tattoos boys noisy children bananas pink hair piercings

The simple present – negative statements

1. We don't like smelly cheese!
Fill in 'don't' or 'doesn't' and the verb.

a. I ______________________ (like) pizza. Hamburgers are much better.

b. Charly and Bill ______________________ (play) tennis every Sunday. They watch football.

c. No, Lisa! ______________________ (watch) TV now! Do your homework, please.

d. Michelle ______________________ (go) shopping in London. It's too noisy.

e. No, we ______________________ (play) on the PC every day. It's boring.

f. Some hamsters ______________________ (sleep) at night. They dance and sing!

2. It's all wrong!
Correct the sentences. The underlined words are wrong.

Example: ***Lisa loves her <u>hamster John</u>. (cat Lindsay)***
No! Lisa doesn't love her hamster John. She loves her cat Lindsay.

a. Rabbits eat <u>steak</u>. – No! ____

____.

b. You drink <u>beer</u> every morning. – No! ____

____.

c. I love <u>chocolate</u> for breakfast. – No! ____

____.

d. We go ice skating in <u>summer</u>. – No! ____

____.

e. Alex <u>reads a book</u> every night. – No! ____

____.

3. About you and your family
Write seven sentences about what your family doesn't like in your exercise book.
You can use the words from the box or other words.

Example: ***My grandfather doesn't like tattoos.***

My mother My parents I My brother / sister My cousins My grandmother My uncle My aunt We My father	**not / like**	cats fish Mondays cheese rats tattoos noisy children bananas pink hair piercings

The simple present – questions with 'do' *

1. Do you speak English?
Setze **do** oder **does** in die Lücken ein.

Example: ***Does Charly go to school?***
Yes, he does. He goes to school every day.

a. __________ you live in England? – No, I don't. I live in Germany.

b. Hey Mum, __________ I look pretty in this dress? – Yes, you do. You look great!

c. __________ the Tribbianis speak Spanish, Dad? – No, they don't. They speak Italian.

d. __________ Lindsay like fish? – Yes, she does. Lindsay eats a lot of fish.

2. Yes, I do!
a. Bringe die Wörter in die richtige Reihenfolge, um sinnvolle Fragen zu bilden.
b. Vervollständige die Kurzantworten mit **do**, **don't**, **does** oder **doesn't**.

Example: ***Minnie Mouse – does – in Disney World – live***
Does Minnie Mouse live in Disney World? – Yes, she does.

a. your father – a musical instrument – play – does
______________________________? – Yes, he ______________.

b. in a flat – you – do – live
______________________________? – No, I ______________.

c. do – your grandfather – does – sport
______________________________? – No, he ______________.

d. a lot of sweets – does – your mother – eat
______________________________? – Yes, she ______________.

3. Interview your classmates.
a. Zeichne wie im Beispiel unten eine Interviewbox in dein Heft.
Überlege dir mithilfe des unteren Kastens fünf Fragen und trage sie in deine Box ein.
b. Stelle drei Mitschülern die Interviewfragen und notiere ihre Antworten.

Interviewbox			
	Answers from student 1	**Answers from student 2**	**Answers from student 3**
1. Do you like chocolate?	Yes, I do.	No, I don't. I ...	Yes, I do. I ...
2. Does your brother ...	No, he doesn't.	Yes, he ...	...
...	...	...	...

Do Does	you your brother your PE teacher your classmates your sister your hamster	love cheeseburgers kiss your dog sleep at night play basketball like chocolate live in your house	?

The simple present – questions with 'do' **

1. Do you speak English?
'Do' or 'Does'? Fill in the gaps.

a. __________ you live in England? – No, I don't. I live in Germany.

b. Hey Mum, __________ I look pretty in this dress? – Yes, you do. You look great!

c. __________ the Tribbianis speak Spanish, Dad? – No, they don't. They speak Italian.

d. __________ Lindsay like fish? – Yes, she does. Lindsay eats a lot of fish.

2. Yes, I do!
a. Put the words in the correct order and write down the questions.
b. Complete the short answers. Look at the example.

Example: ***Minnie Mouse – does – in Disney World – live***
Does Minnie Mouse live in Disney World? – Yes, she does.

a. your father – a musical instrument – play – does

______________________________? – Yes, ______________.

b. in a flat – you – do – live

______________________________? – No, ______________.

c. do – your grandfather – does – sport

______________________________? – No, ______________.

d. a lot of sweets – does – your mother – eat

______________________________? – Yes, ______________.

e. help – your mum – do – you – in the kitchen

______________________________? – No, ______________.

3. Interview your classmates!
a. Draw an interview box like the one below in your exercise book. Think of seven questions and write them into your interview box.
You can use the words from the box at the bottom of the page.
b. Interview three classmates and write down the answers.

Interviewbox			
	Answers from student 1	**Answers from student 2**	**Answers from student 3**
1. Do you like chocolate?	Yes, I do.	No, I don't. I ...	Yes, I do. I ...
2. Does your brother ...	No, he doesn't.	Yes, he ...	...
...	...	...	...

your PE teacher	you	like chocolate	love cheesburgers
your classmates	your brother	live in your house	kiss your dog
your hamster	your mum	play basketball	sleep at night

The simple present – questions with 'do'

1. Do you speak English?
'Do' or 'Does'? Fill in the gaps.

a. __________ you live in England? – No, I __________. I live in Germany.

b. Hey Mum, __________ I look pretty in this dress? – Yes, you __________. You look great!

c. __________ the Tribbianis speak Spanish, Dad? – No, they __________. They speak Italian.

d. __________ Lindsay like fish? – Yes, she __________. Lindsay eats a lot of fish.

e. Hello Michelle, __________ Bill work in the garden a lot? – Yes, he __________. Bill loves flowers.

2. Yes, I do!

a. Put the words in the right order and (circle) the correct verb form. Then write down the questions with the correct form of 'do'.
b. Complete the short answers. Look at the example.

Example: ***Minnie Mouse – do / (does) – in Disney World – live***
Does Minnie Mouse live in Disney World? – Yes, she does.

a. your father – a musical instrument – play – do / does

______________________________? – Yes, ______________.

b. in a flat – you – do / does – live

______________________________? – No, ______________.

c. do – your grandfather – do / does – sport

______________________________? – No, ______________.

d. a lot of sweets – do / does – your mother – eat

______________________________? – Yes, ______________.

e. help – your mum – do / does – you – in the kitchen

______________________________? – No, ______________.

3. Interview your classmates.

a. Draw an interview box like the one below in your exercise book. Think of nine questions and write them into your interview box.
b. Interview four classmates and write down the answers.

Interviewbox				
	Answers from student 1	**Answers from student 2**	**Answers from student 3**	**Answers from student 4**
1. Do you like chocolate?	Yes, I do.	No, I don't. I ...	...	...
2. Does your brother ...	No, he ...	...	...	...
...	...	...	...	...

The simple present – questions with question words

*****

1. What? When? Why?
Trage die Antworten aus dem Kasten unter dem passenden Fragewort in dein Heft ein.

In London. **Because he's from England.** **My friend Kim.** **At school.** **My teacher.** **Great!** **By bike.** **At ten o'clock.** **Because she's nice.** ~~**On Tuesdays.**~~

How?	When?	Where?	Who?	Why?
	On Tuesdays.			

2. What do you play?
Setze die Fragewörter aus dem Kasten in die Lücken ein.

where	how
who	when

Example: ***Where do you watch TV? – I watch TV in my room.***

a. ________ do you live? – I live in London.

b. __________ do you go to bed? – I go to bed at 8 o'clock.

c. ________ do you get to school? – I get to school by bus.

d. __________ is your best friend? – My best friend is Kim.

3. When do you get up?
Bringe die Wörter in die richtige Reihenfolge.

Example: ***(you – do – get up)***
When do you get up? – I get up at 7 o'clock.

a. (Mr. Marty – live – does)
Where ______________________________________? – Mr. Marty lives in London.

b. (to school – Charly – get – does)
How ____? – Charly gets to school by bike.

c. (on Sundays – do – your brother – does)
What _______________________________________? – On Sundays my brother plays football.

4. Ask your partner.
a. Überlege dir mithilfe des Kastens vier Fragen für deine(n) Sitznachbarin/Sitznachbarn. Schreibe die Fragen in dein Heft und lasse Platz für die Antworten.
b. Führe dein Interview durch und notiere die Antworten wie im Beispiel in dein Heft.

Example: ***What does your sister do on Sundays? – On Sundays my sister sleeps.***

What When How Where	do your friends do you do your parents does your sister does your hamster does your grandmother	eat for breakfast? do on Sundays? get to work? sleep? watch TV? get to school? live?

The simple present – questions with question words

*** ***

1. What? When? Why?

Write the answers in the correct list in your exercise book.

In London. Because he's from England. My friend Kim. Horses. My teacher. Great! By bike. At ten o'clock. Because she's nice. ~~On Tuesdays.~~ At school. Pizza. Last week. Ten years old.

How?	When?	Where?	Who?	Why?	What?
	On Tuesdays.				

2. What do you play?

Fill in the correct question words from the grey box.

where	**how**
what	**when**
who	**why**

Example: ***What do you play every day? – I play football every day.***

a. ________ do you live? – I live in London.

b. __________ do you go to bed? – I go to bed at 8 o'clock.

c. ________ do you get to school? – I get to school by bus.

d. __________ is your best friend? – My best friend is Kim.

e. __________ do you like Kim? – I like Kim because she's nice.

f. __________ is your favourite colour? – My favourite colour is green.

3. When do you get up?

Put the words in the correct order.

Example: ***you – when – do – get up***
When do you get up? – I get up at 7 o'clock.

a. Mr. Marty – live – does – where

____? – Mr. Marty lives in London.

b. to school – Charly – get – how – does

____? – Charly gets to school by bike.

c. on Sundays – do – your brother – does – what

____? – On Sundays my brother plays football.

4. Ask your partner.

a. Think of five interview questions with question words and write them into your exercise book. Look at the example question.

b. Interview your partner and write down her/his answers.

Example: ***Where do your parents sleep? – My parents sleep in their bed.***

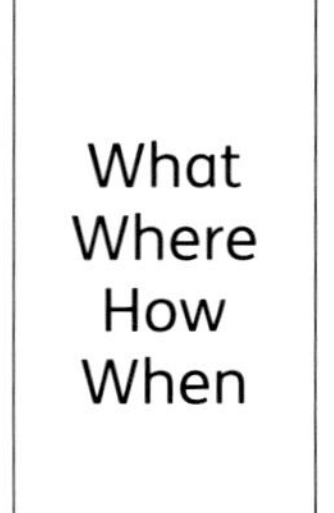

\+

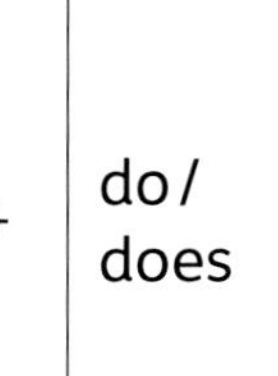

\+

you
your hamster
your grandmother
your friends
your parents
your sister

\+

eat for breakfast?
do on Sundays?
get to work?
sleep?
watch TV?
get to school?
live?

The simple present – questions with question words

1. What? When? Why?

Write the answers in the correct list in your exercise book.

In London. Because he's from England. My friend Kim. Horses. My teacher. Great! By bike. At ten o'clock. Because she's nice. On Tuesdays. At school. Pizza. Last week. Ten years old. Sunny and warm. My mum. In Spain.

How?	When?	Where?	Who?	Why?	What?

2. What do you play?

Fill in the correct question words.

Example: ***Where do you watch TV? – I watch TV in my room.***

a. ________ do you live? – I live in London.

b. __________ do you go to bed? – I go to bed at 8 o'clock.

c. ________ do you get to school? – I get to school by bus.

d. __________ is your best friend? – My best friend is Kim.

e. __________ do you like Kim? – I like Kim because she's nice.

f. __________ is your favourite colour? – My favourite colour is green.

g. __________ is your grandmother? – She's fine.

h. __________ 's going on? – Nothing.

3. When do you get up?

Put the words in the correct order.

a. Mr. Marty – live – does – where

____? – Mr. Marty lives in London.

b. to school – Charly – get – how – does

____? – Charly gets to school by bike.

c. on Sundays – do – your brother – does – what

____? – On Sundays my brother plays football.

d. do – basketball – why – you – play

____? – I play basketball because it's fun.

4. Ask your partner.

a. Think of five interview questions with question words and write them into your exercise book. Look at the example question.

b. Interview your partner and write down her/his answers.

Example: ***When does your hamster watch TV?*** ***– My hamster watches TV every day.***
Who is your best friend? ***– ...***
Why do you ...? ***– ...***

Adverbs of frequency

*****

1. Mr. Marty always cleans his glasses

Setze die Wörter in den Klammern in die richtige Reihenfolge.

Example: ***(his glasses – cleans – always)***
Mr. Marty always cleans his glasses at the end of the lesson.

a. (do – my homework – always)

I ______________________________ at the weekend.

b. (the flowers – waters – often)

Bill ______________________________ at night.

c. (late – get up – usually)

Lisa and Charly ______________________________ on Sundays.

d. (go – to church – sometimes)

We ______________________________ on Christmas.

e. (me – help – never)

You ______________________________ with the cooking.

2. Lindsay never makes pancakes

Sieh dir den Kasten an und schreibe:
a. drei Sätze über Lindsay und **b.** drei Sätze über dich selbst.

Lindsay...	never	often	usually	always
~~(wash the car)~~	X			
(watch TV)		X		
(be nice)				X
(sleep on the sofa)			X	

a. ***Lindsay never washes the car.***

____

____

____

b. ***I sometimes wash the car.***

____

____

____

3. About your family

Schreibe vier Sätze über deine Familie oder dich in dein Heft. Du kannst die Wörter aus dem Kasten verwenden.

I My parents My sister My brother My grandmother My grandfather	sometimes never usually often always	read books tidy up the living room go shopping use a smartphone take out the rubbish write e-mails

Example: ***My sister sometimes writes e-mails.***

Adverbs of frequency

*** ***

1. Mr. Marty always cleans his glasses

Put the words in the correct order.

Example:
his glasses – at the end of the lesson –
Mr. Marty – cleans – always
Mr. Marty always cleans his glasses at the end of the lesson.

a. do – at the weekend – my homework – I – always

____

b. the flowers – Bill – waters – at night – often

____

c. late – on Sundays – get up – Lisa and Charly – usually

____

d. go – on Christmas – to church – sometimes – we

____

e. you – with the cooking – me – help – never

____

2. Lindsay never makes pancakes

Look at the box: **a.** Write four sentences about Lindsay.
b. What about you? Write four sentences.

Lindsay …	never	sometimes	often	usually	always
(wash the car)	X				
(watch TV)			X		
(is nice)					X
(sleep on the sofa)				X	
(drink milk)		X			

a. ***Lindsay never washes the car.***

____
____
____
____

b. ***I sometimes wash the car.***

____
____
____
____

3. About your family

Write five sentences about your family in your exercise book.

Example: ***My sister sometimes writes e-mails.***

I My sister My dog My mum	My brother My grandmother My cat	+	sometimes never usually	always often	+	…

Adverbs of frequency

* * *

1. Mr. Marty always cleans his glasses
Translate the German word in brackets into English und put the words in the right order.

Example:
of the lesson – his glasses – at the end – Mr. Marty – cleans – (immer)
Mr. Marty always cleans his glasses at the end of the lesson.

a. do – the weekend – my homework – I – (immer) – at

b. the flowers – Bill – at – waters – night – (oft)

c. late – Sundays – get up – Lisa and Charly – (normalerweise) – on

d. to – go – on Christmas – church – (manchmal) – we

e. you – the cooking – me – help – (nie) – with

2. Lindsay never makes pancakes
Look at the box: **a.** Write five sentences about Lindsay.
b. What about you? Write five sentences.

Lindsay ...	never	sometimes	often	usually	always
(wash the car)	X				
(watch TV)			X		
(is nice)					X
(sleep on the sofa)				X	
(drink milk)		X			

a. Lindsay ...

b. I ...

c. Think of one more activity and write one sentence about Lindsay and one about yourself.

3. About your family
Write six sentences about your family in your exercise book. You can use the words from the box or other adverbs of frequency.

sometimes never often usually always

Example: ***My sister sometimes writes e-mails.***

Object pronouns

*****

1. Help me!

Unterstreiche in den Sätzen die Objektpronomen. Ordne den Sätzen dann die passenden Bilder zu, indem du die Bildnummer einträgst.

a. Mr. Marty, can you help me? – That's picture ______.

b. Oh, no! I have to clean it. – That's picture ______.

c. She's pretty. I love her. – That's picture ______.

d. Mum, we're hungry. Can you make us a sandwich, please? – That's picture ______.

e. Ugghh! These boots are terrible. I hate them. – That's picture ______.

2. I can't see them.

Trage in die Lücken die passenden Objektformen aus dem Kasten ein.

~~it~~ you (2x) them him her me

Example: ***Can you see the small mouse? – No, I can't see it.***

a. Where do we write down the answers? – Write __________ down here, please.

b. I'm in the room next door. You can call __________, if you need help.

c. Dear students, today I want to give __________ your tests back.

d. These wonderful flowers are from Bill. – Wow! Don't forget to thank __________.

e. Lindsay, I can't see __________. Where are you?

f. Where's Michelle? I want to help __________ in the garden.

3. Listen to him.

Bringe die Wörter in die richtige Reihenfolge, um sinnvolle Sätze zu erhalten. Die Satzanfänge und Satzenden helfen dir.

Example: ***help – us – can – you*** ➡ ***Can you help us, Mr. Webber?***

a. (love – I – them)

Donuts are great. ____

b. (you – me – bring – can)

Hey Santa Claus, ______________________________ many presents, please?

c. (repair – it – you – can)

Oh no! The car is broken. ______________________________, Mr. Webber?

d. (him – listen to – please)

Ssshhh! Mr. Marty wants to tell us something. ______________________________

Object pronouns

*** ***

1. Help me!
a. Match the pictures with the sentences by writing the correct picture number in the gap.
b. Circle the correct object pronoun!

a. Mr. Marty, can you help **them / me**? – That's picture ______.

b. Oh, no! I have to clean **her / it**. – That's picture ______.

c. She's pretty. I love **me / her**. – That's picture ______.

d. Mum, we're hungry. Can you make **us / you** a sandwich, please? – That's picture ______.

e. Ugghh! These boots are terrible. I hate **them / him**. – That's picture ______.

2. I can't see them.
a. Fill in the gaps with the correct object pronouns from the grey box.
b. Which word belongs to the object pronoun? Underline it.

it
you (2x)
them
him
her
me

Example: ***Can you see the small mouse? – No, I can't see it.***

a. Where do we write down the answers? – Write __________ down here, please.

b. I'm in the room next door. You can call __________, if you need help.

c. Dear students, today I want to give __________ your tests back.

d. These wonderful flowers are from Bill. – Wow! Don't forget to thank __________.

e. Lindsay, I can't see __________. Where are you?

f. Where's Michelle? I want to help __________ in the garden.

3. Listen to him.
Put the words in the correct order. The sentence beginnings (and endings) help you.

Example: ***help – us – can – you*** ➡ ***Can you help us, Mr. Webber?***

a. are – love – I – them – great

Donuts ____

b. you – me – bring – can – many presents

Hey Santa Claus, ____, please?

c. broken – repair – it – is – you – can

Oh no! The car ____, Mr. Webber?

d. him – something – listen to – please – us

Ssshhh! Mr. Marty wants to tell ____

Object pronouns

1. Help me!

a. Match the pictures with the sentences by writing the correct picture number in the gap.
b. Fill in the correct object pronouns: **me**, **you**, **her**, **him**, **it**, **them** or **us**.

a. Mr. Marty, can you help __________? – That's picture ______.

b. Oh, no! I have to clean __________. – That's picture ______.

c. She's pretty. I love __________. – That's picture ______.

d. Mum, we're hungry. Can you make __________ a sandwich, please? – That's picture ______.

e. Ugghh! These boots are terrible. I hate __________. – That's picture ______.

2. I can't see them!

a. Fill in the gaps with the correct object forms.
b. Which word belongs to the object form? Underline it.

Example: ***Can you see the small mouse? – No, I can't see it.***

a. Where do we write down the answers? – Write __________ down here, please.

b. I'm in the room next door. You can call __________, if you need help.

c. Dear students, today I want to give __________ your tests back.

d. These wonderful flowers are from Bill. – Wow! Don't forget to thank __________.

e. Lindsay, I can't see __________. Where are you?

f. Where's Michelle? I want to help __________ in the garden.

3. Listen to him!

Put the words in the correct order. The sentence beginnings (and endings) help you.

Example: ***help – us – can – you ➡ Can you help us, Mr. Webber?***

a. are – love – I – them – great
Donuts ______________________________. ______________________________.

b. you – me – bring – can – many presents
Hey Santa Claus, ____, please?

c. broken – repair – it – is – you – can
Oh no! The car ______________________________. ______________________________, Mr. Webber?

d. him – something – listen to – please – us
Ssshhh! Mr. Marty wants to tell ______________________. ______________________.

e. mad – her – talk to – at you – is
Lisa ______________________________. ______________________________, Charly.

Quantifiers: some and any

*

1. Can I have some juice, please?
Trage **some** oder **any** in die Lücken ein.

Examples: ***I've got some money under my bed.***
There aren't any sweets in the house.

a. Have we got __________ good books?

b. There's __________ cheese in the fridge.

c. Would you like __________ ice in your lemonade?

d. They are poor and haven't got __________ money.

2. Lisa's birthday presents
Schau dir das Bild an und schreibe vier Sätze darüber, was Lisa auf ihrem Geburtstagstisch hat oder nicht hat.

Lisa *hasn't got any* dresses.

Lisa *has got some* chocolate.

Lisa ____________________ sweets.

Lisa ____________________ money.

Lisa ____________________ magazines.

Lisa ____________________ T-shirts.

3. I haven't got any money in my room.
Schreibe fünf Sätze über dein Zimmer. Benutze die Wörter aus dem Kasten.

I	have got haven't	some any	books toys	sweets posters	pens clothes	curtains pets	in my room.

____

____

____

____

____

____

Quantifiers: some and any

1. Can I have some juice, please?
Put in 'some' or 'any'.

Examples: ***I've got some money under my bed.***
There aren't any sweets in the house.

a. Have we got __________ good books?
b. There's __________ cheese in the fridge.
c. Would you like __________ ice in your lemonade?
d. They are poor and haven't got __________ money.
e. Oh no! I haven't got __________ nice clothes!
f. Is there __________ milk? – No, but there's __________ water.

2. Lisa's birthday presents
Look at Lisa's birthday table and write seven sentences.

sweets magazines board games T-shirts money concert tickets ~~dresses~~ ~~chocolate~~ books

Lisa hasn't got any dresses.
Lisa has got some chocolate.
Lisa hasn't got ______________________________

____

____

____

____

____

____

3. I haven't got any money in my room.
Write six sentences about your room. You can use the words from the box.

books sweets pens curtains toys posters clothes pets

Start like this: ***I haven't got any ... in my room.***
I have got some ...

____

____

____

____

____

____

____

Quantifiers: some and any

* * *

1. Can I have some juice, please?
Put in 'some' or 'any'.

a. Have we got __________ good books?

b. There's __________ cheese in the fridge.

c. Would you like __________ ice in your lemonade?

d. They are poor and haven't got __________ money.

e. Oh no! I haven't got __________ nice clothes!

f. Is there __________ milk? – No, but there's __________ water.

g. Oh no! I don't see __________ food in the fridge and I'm very hungry.

h. Can we have __________ chocolate later, Mum?

2. Lisa's birthday presents
Look at Lisa's birthday table and write eleven sentences in your exercise book.

Lisa hasn't got any dresses.

Lisa has got ______________________________

pens magazines board games T-shirts money concert tickets ~~dresses~~ chocolate books sweets caps make-up

3. I haven't got any money in my room.
Write seven sentences about your room.

***Start like this:** I haven't got any … in my room.*
I have got some …

Quantifiers: much and many

*

1. Mum! I'm hungry!
Trage **much** oder **many** in die Lücken ein. Beachte die Hilfestellung im Kasten.

You use **much** for uncountable nouns: water, money, bread, butter ...
You use **many** for countable nouns: books, cars, dogs, bananas ...

Michelle: Have you got ___*much*___ homework today?
Lisa: Yes, we have to learn so ___*many*___ words for English – it's too ________ work. I'm hungry. Can I have something to eat?
Michelle: Mmmmhh, we haven't got ________ food here.
Lisa: Oh, no! Let's write a shopping list.
Michelle: I'm sorry. I haven't got ________ time. Can you do it?
Lisa: OK. How ________ apples are there?
Michelle: There's one old apple.
Lisa: How ____________ chocolate do we need?
Michelle: We don't need chocolate, but we haven't got ____________ milk in the fridge.
Lisa: All right ... so we need milk and apples. That's not ________.
Michelle: Write down butter, bread, watermelons ...
Lisa: How ____________ watermelons?
Michelle: Two watermelons, please.

2. What's in the picture?
Sieh dir das Bild an und schreibe fünf Sätze mit **much** und **many** in dein Heft. Benutze folgende Nomen:

1. water – 2. muffins – 3. biscuits
4. sugar – 5. strawberries

Examples: ***(money) → There isn't much money.***
(apples) → There aren't many apples.

SUGAR
WATER

3. Interview your partner.
a. Von welchen Dingen gibt es bei deiner Sitznachbarin/deinem Sitznachbarn viel zu Hause? Schreibe vier Fragen mit **much** und **many** in dein Heft. Benutze die Wörter aus dem Kasten.
b. Führe das Interview durch und notiere die Antworten.

Examples: ***Have you got much coffee at home? – Yes, we have.***
Have you got many lamps at home? – No, we haven't.

chocolate ~~**coffee**~~ **fun** **books** ~~**lamps**~~ **plates**

Quantifiers: much and many

1. Mum! I'm hungry!
Put in **'much'** or **'many'**.

Michelle: Have you got ***much*** homework today?

Lisa: Yes, we have to learn so ***many*** words for English – it's too ________ work. I'm hungry. Can I have something to eat?

Michelle: Mmmmhh, we haven't got ________ food here.

Lisa: Oh, no! Let's write a shopping list.

Michelle: I'm sorry. I haven't got ________ time. Can you do it?

Lisa: OK. How ________ apples are there?

Michelle: There's one old apple.

Lisa: How ____________ chocolate do we need?

Michelle: We don't need chocolate, but we haven't got ____________ milk in the fridge.

Lisa: All right ... so we need milk and apples. That's not ________.

Michelle: Write down butter, bread, watermelons ...

Lisa: How ____________ watermelons?

Michelle: Two watermelons, please. Oh, and there isn't ____________ cat food. Write that down too.

Lisa: OK. Come on! Let's go! Shopping is so ________ fun.

2. What's in the picture?
Look at the picture and the words.
Write seven sentences in your exercise book and use 'much' or 'many'.

1. water – 2. muffins – 3. biscuits – 4. sugar
5. strawberries – 6. cheese – 7. carrots

Examples: ***(money) ➞ There isn't much money.***
(apples) ➞ There aren't many apples.

3. Interview your partner.

a. Has your partner got much milk or many pets at home? Write down five interview questions and use 'much' and 'many'. You can use the words from the box or other words.

b. Interview your partner and write down the answers.

Example: ***Have you got many bananas at home? – Yes, we have.***

chocolate coffee cheese noise lamps beer
chairs TVs plates books butter ~~bananas~~

Quantifiers: much and many

1. Mum! I'm hungry!
Put in **'much'** or **'many'**.

Michelle: Have you got ***much*** homework today?

Lisa: Yes, we have to learn so ***many*** words for English – it's too ________ work. I'm hungry. Can I have something to eat?

Michelle: Mmmmhh, we haven't got ________ food here.

Lisa: Oh, no! Let's write a shopping list.

Michelle: I'm sorry. I haven't got ________ time. Can you do it?

Lisa: OK. How ________ apples are there?

Michelle: There's one old apple.

Lisa: How ____________ chocolate do we need?

Michelle: We don't need chocolate, but we haven't got ____________ milk in the fridge.

Lisa: All right ... so we need milk and apples. That's not ________.

Michelle: Write down butter, bread, watermelons ...

Lisa: How ____________ watermelons?

Michelle: Two watermelons, please. Oh, and there isn't ____________ cat food. Write that down too.

Lisa: OK. Come on! Let's go! Shopping is so __________ fun.

Michelle: Well ... I think shopping food isn't ______ fun at all. There are too ________ people and too ________ noise.

2. What's in the picture?
Look at the picture. Write seven sentences in your exercise book and use 'much' or 'many'.

Examples: ***There <u>isn't much money</u>.***
There <u>aren't many apples</u>.

3. Interview your partner.

a. Has your partner got much milk or many pets at home? Write down six interview questions and use 'much' and 'many'.

b. Interview your partner and write down the answers.

Example: ***Have you got many bananas at home? – Yes, we have.***

The present progressive – positive and negative statements 

1. A mouse in Birdhurst Road?

Ergänze die passende Form von „to be“: am – is – are.

It's 9 o'clock on a Saturday and the Webbers ___*are*___ sitting in the kitchen. Bill __________ reading the newspaper. Lisa ________ doing something on her phone. Michelle says, "Where's Charly?" No answer ... "Hello? Listen to me, please. Where's Charly?" she shouts. Lisa says, "Sorry, Mum. I __________ texting with Alex. Charly and Lindsay are upstairs. They __________ looking for the mouse." Bill screams, "What? I can't believe a mouse ____________ living on in my house. I hate mice!" Then Charly and Lindsay come into the kitchen. Lindsay ________ carrying something grey in her mouth. "Ugghhh!" Bill shouts and jumps on the table. "Relax, Dad. It's just a toy mouse," Charly says. Michelle and Lisa ______ laughing out loud.

2. What are they doing?

Schreibe auf, was auf dem Bild gerade getan wird.

a. ~~Hamster Donald~~		playing	~~in his cage.~~
b. I	**'m**	watching	a nice book.
c. Bill	**is**	drinking	a board game.
d. We	**are**	reading	some milk.
e. Cat Lindsay		~~sleeping~~	TV.

a. ***Hamster Donald*** ***is*** ***sleeping*** ***in his cage.***

b. ____.

c. ____.

d. ____.

e. ____.

3. No, I'm not eating your pizza!

Die unterstrichenen Wörter sind falsch. Richtig ist, was in in den Klammern steht. Schreibe die korrigierten Sätze in dein Heft.

Example: ***Superman is <u>sleeping</u>. (read a comic)***
Superman isn't sleeping. ➜ He's reading a comic.

a. Alex is flirting with hamster Donald. (Lisa)
b. Our grandparents are sleeping. (play on the PC)
c. I'm drinking a beer. (a cup of tea)
d. You are dancing. (sing)

The present progressive – positive and negative statements

1. A mouse in Birdhurst Road?
Fill in the correct form of 'to be' and the *-ing* form of the verb.

It's 9 o'clock on a Saturday and the Webbers ***are sitting*** sitting in the kitchen. Bill ________________ (read) the newspaper. Lisa ________________ (do) something on her phone. Michelle says, "Where's Charly?" No answer … "Hello? Listen to me, please. Where's Charly?" she shouts. Lisa says "Sorry, Mum. I ________________ (text) with Alex. Charly and Lindsay are upstairs. They ________________ (look) for the mouse." Bill screams, "What? I can't believe a mouse ________________ (live) in my house. I hate mice!" Then Charly and Lindsay come into the kitchen. Lindsay ________________ (carry) something grey in her mouth. "Ugghhh!" Bill shouts and jumps on the table. "Relax, Dad. It's just a toy mouse," Charly says. Michelle and Lisa ________________ (laugh) out loud.

2. What are they doing?
Look at the picture and write down what they are doing.

play	~~in his cage.~~
watch	a nice book.
drink	a board game.
eat	some milk.
read	TV.
~~sleep~~	cheese.

a. ***Hamster Donald is sleeping in his cage.***

b. I ________________________________.

c. Bill ________________________________.

d. We ________________________________.

e. Cat Lindsay ________________________________.

f. Two mice ________________________________.

3. No, I'm not eating your pizza!
a. Fill in the gaps with the correct form of 'to be'.
b. The underlined words are wrong. Correct the sentences with the words in brackets and write them in your exercise book.

Example: ***Superman is sleeping. (read a comic) → Superman isn't sleeping. He's reading a comic.***

a. Alex ________ flirting with hamster Donald. (Lisa)

b. Our grandparents ________ sleeping. (play on the PC)

c. I ________ drinking a beer. (a cup of tea)

d. You ________ dancing. (sing)

The present progressive – positive and negative statements

1. A mouse in Birdhurst Road?
Fill in the correct present progressive form of the verb.

It's 9 o'clock on a Saturday and the Webbers __________ (sit) in the kitchen. Bill __________ (read) the newspaper. Lisa __________ (do) something on her phone. Michelle says, "Where's Charly?" No answer ..."Hello? Listen to me, please. Where's Charly?" she shouts. Lisa says "Sorry, Mum. I __________ (text) with Alex. Charly and Lindsay are upstairs. They __________ (look) for the mouse." Bill screams, "What? I can't believe a mouse __________ (live) in my house. I hate mice!" Then Charly and Lindsay come into the kitchen. Lindsay __________ (carry) something grey in her mouth. "Ugghhh!" Bill shouts and jumps on the table. "Relax, Dad. It's just a toy mouse," Charly says. Michelle and Lisa __________ (laugh) out loud. "That's not funny!" Bill shouts. "Relax, Sweetheart. I think it's funny. Ehhh ... What ______ Donald ______ (do) there?" says Michelle. "He __________ (eat) your favourite chocolate, Mum," Lisa anwers. "Oh no!!" Michelle screams. Bill smiles and says, "Relax, Sweet-heart. I think, it's funny."

2. What are they doing?
Look at the picture and write down what they are doing.

a. ***Hamster Donald is sleeping in his cage.***
b. I __________________________.
c. Bill __________________________.
d. We __________________________.
e. Cat Lindsay __________________________.
f. Two mice __________________________.
g. You __________________________.

3. No, I'm not eating your pizza!
a. Fill in the gaps with the correct form of 'to be'.
b. The underlined words are wrong. Correct the sentences with the words in brackets and write them in your exercise book.

Example: ***Superman is sleeping. (read a comic) → Superman isn't sleeping. He's reading a comic.***

a. Alex ________ flirting with hamster Donald. (Lisa)
b. Our grandparents ________ sleeping. (play on the PC)
c. I ________ drinking a beer. (a cup of tea)
d. You ________ dancing. (sing)
e. We ________ eating hamsters. (frogs)
f. Lindsay ________ sleeping on the sofa. (in Lisa's bed)

The present progressive – questions

*****

1. Are you eating my ice cream?

Ergänze in den Fragen die passende Form von ‚to be' und die *-ing*-Form des Verbs. Die Antworten helfen dir.

Example: ***Charly, <u>are</u> you <u>eating</u> my ice cream? (eat)***
– No, I'm not eating your ice cream. I'm eating dad's ice cream.

a. ______ Lindsay ________________ in my bed again? (sleep) – No, she isn't sleeping in your bed. She's sleeping in Charly's bed.

b. ______ I ________________ good in this jeans, Bill? (look) – Yes, you are looking great, Michelle.

c. ______ the kids ____________________ TV? (watch) – Yes, they are watching the news.

2. Where are you going, young man?

Vervollständige die Fragen. Die Bilder und die Antworten helfen dir.

Example: ***Where are you going, young man?*** ***– I'm going to school, Mum.***	a. What ____________ Charly ________________ – Charly is watching a funny DVD.	b. Who ________________ Jingle Bells? – Mr. Marty is singing Jingle Bells.
c. How __________ Michelle __________ her muffins? – Michelle is making them with blueberries.	d. Why ______________ Lisa ____________________? – Lisa is crying because of Alex.	e. Where ____ the Johnsons ____________ on holiday? – The Johnsons are going on holiday to Spain.

3. Now you

a. Schreibe mithilfe des Kastens vier Fragen für deine(n) Sitznachbarin / Sitznachbarn in dein Heft. Lasse unter den Fragen Platz für eine Antwort.

b. Interviewe deine(n) Sitznachbarin / Sitznachbarn und notiere ihre / seine Antworten.

Am Is Are	your friend you ~~the sun~~ ~~our teacher~~ the classroom it your grandparents I your dog	wearing jeans? feeling good? working at the moment? raining outside? sitting on a chair? ~~shining today?~~ ~~reading something?~~ looking nice and tidy?

Examples:
Is our teacher reading something?
– No, he isn't. He's helping a student.

Is the sun shining today? – Yes, it is.

The present progressive – questions

1. Are you eating my ice cream?
Fill in the correct form of 'to be' and the *-ing* form of the verb.

Example: ***Charly, are you eating my ice cream? (eat)***
– No, I'm not eating your ice cream. I'm eating dad's ice cream.

a. ______ Lindsay ________________ in my bed again? (sleep) – No, she ________________ in your bed. She's sleeping in Charly's bed.

b. ______ I ________________ good in this jeans, Bill? (look) – Yes, you ________________ great, Michelle.

c. ______ the kids ________________ TV? (watch) – Yes, they ________________ the news.

2. Where are you going, young man?
Complete the questions. The pictures and the answers help you. You have to ask for the underlined words.

Example: ***Where are you going, young man?*** ***– I'm going to school, Mum.***	a. What ________________ ________________? – Charly is watching a funny DVD.	b. Who ________________ ________________? – Mr. Marty is singing Jingle Bells.
c. How ________________ ________________? – Michelle is making them with blueberries.	d. Why ________________ ________________? – Lisa is crying because of Alex.	e. Where ________________ ________________? – The Johnsons are going on holiday to Spain.

3. Now you
a. Write down five questions in the present progressive for your partner in your exercise book. Leave some space for the answers. You can use the words from the box.
b. Interview your partner and write down the answers.

your friend you ~~the sun~~ ~~our teacher~~ the classroom it your dad I your dog	sit on a chair feel good work at the moment rain outside wear jeans ~~shine today~~ ~~read something~~ look nice and tidy

Examples:
Is our teacher reading something?
– No, he isn't. He's helping a student.

Is the sun shining today? – Yes, it is.

The present progressive – questions

*** * ***

1. Are you eating my ice cream?

Fill in the correct form of 'to be' and the *-ing* form of the verb.

Example: ***Charly, <u>are</u> you <u>eating</u> my ice cream? (eat)***
– No, <u>I'm not eating</u> your ice cream. I<u>'m eating</u> dad's ice cream.

a. ______ Lindsay ______________ in my bed again? (sleep) – No, she ________________ in your bed. She ______________ in Charly's bed.

b. ______ I ______________ good in this jeans, Bill? (look) – Yes, you ________________ great, Michelle.

c. ______ the kids ______________ TV? (watch) – Yes, they ________________ the news.

d. ______ we ______________ pudding for dessert? (have) – No, we ________________ pudding for dessert. We ______________ yogurt.

2. Where are you going, young man?

Write down the questions with the question words from the box. The pictures and the answers help you. You have to ask for the underlined words.

who why what where how

Example: ***Where are you going, young man?*** ***– I'm going <u>to school</u>, Mum.***	a. What ______________ ______________? – Charly is watching <u>a funny DVD</u>.	b. Who ______________ ______________? – <u>Mr. Marty</u> is singing Jingle Bells.
c. How ______________ ______________? – Michelle is making them <u>with blueberries</u>.	d. Why ______________ ______________? – Lisa is crying <u>because of Alex</u>.	e. Where ______________ ______________? – The Johnsons are going on holiday <u>to Spain</u>.

3. Now you

a. Write down six questions in the present progressive for your partner in your exercise book. Leave some space for the answers.

b. Interview your partner and write down the answers.

Examples: ***Is your friend sitting on a chair?*** ***– Yes, he is.***
Is it raining today? ***– No, it isn't.***
Are your classmates sleeping? ***– ...***

The simple past – was / were

*

1. That was a great day!

Trage die passende Form in die Lücken ein: **was / were – wasn't / weren't**

Bill: Hi Charly! How ***was*** (was / were) your day?

Charly: My day ***wasn't*** (wasn't / /weren't) very exciting. Where's mum? __________ (was / were) she here today?

Bill: No, she __________ (wasn't / weren't) here. There __________ (was / were) a concert at Hyde Park. She and Lisa __________ (was / were) at this concert.

Charly: Oh really? What kind of concert __________ (was / were) that? Heavy metal?

Bill: No, it __________ (wasn't / weren't) heavy metal. What __________ (was / were) the name of that little singer again? I can't remember. Oh, now I know! Justin Weeper!

Michelle and Lisa are coming home.

Lisa: This __________ (was / were) the best day of my life. Justin __________ (was / were) so cool and good-looking. And the music __________ (wasn't / weren't) just good – it __________ (was / were) fantastic!

Michelle: I think the music __________ (wasn't / weren't) fantastic at all.
Actually it __________ (was / were) terrible.
And there __________ (was / were) so many fans.

2. Was the test easy?

Bilde zu den Antworten die Fragen, indem du die Wörter in die richtige Reihenfolge bringst.

Example: ***your friend – at school – was → Was your friend at school? – Yes, he was.***

a. there – were – any nice boys
____ at the party? – No, there weren't.

b. your grandfather – at the football match – was
____ yesterday? – Yes, he was.

c. were – in the garden – your parents
____ last weekend? – No, they weren't.

d. you – last week – were
Where ____? – Last week I was in Spain.

e. in Spain – the weather – was
How ____? – It was terrible: Rainy and cold!

3. Interview your partner

a. Überlege dir mithilfe des Kastens für deine(n) Sitznachbarin/Sitznachbarn vier Fragen und schreibe sie in dein Heft. Lasse etwas Platz für die Antworten.

b. Interviewe deine(n) Sitznachbarn/Sitznachbarin und notiere die Antworten.

Example: ***Was your teacher on the moon last Tuesday? – No, he wasn't.***

Were Was	you your pencil case your father your classmates your teacher	on the moon in Paris happy at your football match in the classroom	last Tuesday? in 2016? yesterday? two weeks ago? in April?

The simple past – was / were

*** ***

1. That was a great day!

Fill in the correct form of 'to be': **was / were – wasn't / weren't**

Bill: Hi Charly! How ***was*** (was / were) your day?

Charly: My day __________ (wasn't / weren't) very exciting. Where's mum? __________ (was / were) she here today?

Bill: No, she __________ (wasn't / weren't) here. There __________ (was / were) a concert at Hyde Park. She and Lisa __________ (was / were) at this concert.

Charly: Oh really? What kind of concert __________ (was / were) that? Heavy metal?

Bill: No, it __________ (wasn't / weren't) heavy metal. What __________ (was / were) the name of that little singer again? I can't remember. Oh, now I know! Justin Weeper!

Michelle and Lisa are coming home.

Lisa: This __________ (was / were) the best day of my life. Justin __________ (was / were) so cool and good-looking. And the music __________ (wasn't / weren't) just good – it __________ (was / were) fantastic!

Michelle: I think the music __________ (wasn't / weren't) fantastic at all. Actually it __________ (was / were) terrible.
And there __________ (was / were) so many fans.

Charly: What about Alex? Isn't he your boyfriend, Lisa?

Lisa: Alex __________ (was / were) my boyfriend. It's over. I want Justin now.

2. Was the test easy?

Put the words in the correct order to make questions.

Example: ***your friend – at school – was ➡ Was your friend at school? – Yes, he was.***

a. at the party – there – were – any nice boys

______________________________? – No, there weren't.

b. your grandfather – at the football match – yesterday – was

______________________________? – Yes, he was.

c. were – last weekend – in the garden – your parents

______________________________? – No, they weren't.

d. you – last week – were – where

______________________________? – Last week I was in Spain.

e. in Spain – how – the weather – was

______________________________? – It was terrible: Rainy and cold!

3. Interview your partner

a. Think of five interview questions with 'was' or 'were' for your partner. Write them in your exercise book. Leave some space for the answers. You can use the words from the box.

b. Interview your partner and write down the answers.

Example: ***Was your teacher on the moon last Tuesday? – No, he wasn't.***

you	your parents	on the moon	in Berlin	last Tuesday	on Sunday morning
your pencil case	Santa Claus	happy	at home	in 2016	in April
your classmates	your hamster	at your football match	at a concert	last week	last weekend
your teacher	your friend	in the classroom	shopping	two years ago	yesterday

The simple past – was / were

* * *

1. That was a great day!

Fill in the correct form of 'to be': **was / were** (☺) – **wasn't / weren't** (☹)

Bill: Hi Charly! How ***was*** (☺) your day?

Charly: My day ___________ (☹) very exciting. Where's mum? ___________ (☺) she here today?

Bill: No, she ___________ (☹) here. There ___________ (☺) a concert at Hyde Park. She and Lisa ___________ (☺) at this concert.

Charly: Oh really? What kind of concert ___________ (☺) that? Heavy metal?

Bill: No, it ___________ (☹) heavy metal. What ___________ (☺) the name of that little singer again? I can't remember. Oh, now I know! Justin Weeper!

Michelle and Lisa are coming home.

Lisa: This ___________ (☺) the best day of my life. Justin ___________ (☺) so cool and good-looking. And the music ___________ (☹) just good – it ___________ (☺) fantastic!

Michelle: I think the music ___________ (☹) fantastic at all. Actually it ___________ (☺) terrible. And there ___________ (☺) so many fans.

Charly: What about Alex? Isn't he your boyfriend, Lisa?

Lisa: Alex ___________ (☺) my boyfriend. It's over. I want Justin now.

Bill: Oh dear. When I ___________ (☺) young, there ___________ (☺) some nice singers too.

Lisa: Yeah, right. 100 years ago, everything ___________ (☺) great.

2. Was the test easy?

Put the words in the correct order to make questions. Then look at the answers on the right and fill in the correct form of 'to be'.

Example: ***your friend – at school – was ➡ Was your friend at school? – Yes, he was.***

a. at the party – there – were – any nice boys
____? – No, there ___________.

b. your grandfather – at the football match – yesterday – was
____? – Yes, he ___________.

c. were – last weekend – in the garden – your parents
____? – No, they ___________.

d. you – last week – were – where
____? – Last week I ___________ in Spain.

e. in Spain – how – the weather – was
____? – It ___________ terrible: Rainy and cold!

3. Interview your partner

a. Think of six interview questions with 'was' or 'were' for your partner. Write them in your exercise book. Leave some space for the answers.

b. Interview your partner and write down the answers.

Example: ***Was your teacher on the moon last Tuesday? – No, he wasn't.
Were your classmates in the classroom yesterday? – Yes, they were.***

The simple past (regular verbs) – positive statements 

1. Charly's week

Was hat Charly an den einzelnen Tagen der letzten Woche gemacht? Ergänze das Verb im *simple past*.

Monday	Tuesday	Wednesday	Thursday	Friday
listen to music	play football	talk to his friends	wait	watch TV
Example: ***On Monday Charly*** ***<u>listened</u> to music.***	On Tuesday Charly ______________ ______________.	On Wednesday Charly ______________ ______________.	On Thursday Charly ______________ for the bus.	On Friday Charly ______________ ______________.

2. Granny Grace

Setze die passenden Formen des *simple past* ein.

When I was a young girl, I ***walked*** (walk) one hour to school every morning – even if it ____________ (rain) or ____________ (snow). At school we ____________ (listen) to the teacher all the time. We never ____________ (chat) or ____________ (laugh) in the lesson. After school we ____________ (hurry) home because there was a lot of work to do. I always ____________ (help) my mum in the kitchen. I ____________ (wash) the dishes and ____________ (tidy) the kitchen. When all the work was finished, my father ____________ (play) the piano and we ____________ (dance). We never ____________ (watch) TV or ____________ (look) at smartphones.

3. My weekend

Schreibe vier Sätze über dein letztes Wochenende in dein Heft. Du kannst dafür die Wörter aus dem Kasten verwenden. Denke daran, die Vergangenheitsform der Verben zu benutzen.

Example: ***On Friday afternoon I visited my aunt and my uncle.***

On Friday afternoon On Friday night On Saturday morning On Saturday afternoon On Sunday morning On Sunday afternoon	I my parents my grandparents my sister my brother	chat with play talk to help watch listen to visit	some nice music. football. my aunt and my uncle. TV. my mum in the garden. my friend. on my phone.

The simple past (regular verbs) – positive statements

1. Charly's week

Write sentences about Charly's week. Use the simple past form of the verb.

Monday	Tuesday	Wednesday
 listen to music	 play football	 talk to his friends
Example: ***On Monday Charly listened to music.***	______________	______________
Thursday	**Friday**	**Saturday**
 wait for the bus	 watch TV	 wash the car
______________	______________	______________

2. Granny Grace

Fill in the correct forms of the simple past.

When I was a young girl, I ***walked*** (walk) one hour to school every morning – even if it __________ (rain) or __________ (snow). At school we __________ (listen) to the teacher all the time. We never __________ (chat) or __________ (laugh) in the lesson. After school we __________ (hurry) home because there was a lot of work to do. I always __________ (help) my mum in the kitchen. I __________ (wash) the dishes and __________ (tidy) the kitchen. When all the work was finished, my father __________ (play) the piano and we __________ (dance). We never __________ (watch) TV or __________ (look) at smartphones. We__________ (talk) a lot. We really __________ (love) our family nights.

3. My weekend

Write five sentences about your last weekend in your exercise book.

Examples: ***On Friday afternoon I visited my aunt and my uncle.***
On Friday night my sister ...

The simple past (regular verbs) – positive statements

1. Charly's week

Write sentences about Charly's week. Use the simple past.

Monday	Tuesday	Wednesday
***Example:* On Monday Charly listened to music.**	____________	____________

Thursday	Friday	Saturday
____________	____________	____________

2. Granny Grace

Fill in the correct forms of the simple past.

When I was a young girl, I ***walked*** (walk) one hour to school every morning – even if it ____________ (rain) or ____________ (snow). At school we ____________ (listen) to the teacher all the time. We never ____________ (chat) or ____________ (laugh) in the lesson. After school we ____________ (hurry) home because there was a lot of work to do. I always ____________ (help) my mum in the kitchen. I ____________ (wash) the dishes and ____________ (tidy) the kitchen. When all the work was finished, my father ____________ (play) the piano and we ____________ (dance). We never ____________ (watch) TV or ____________ (look) at smartphones. We____________ (talk) a lot. We really ____________ (love) our family nights. Last year I __________ (start) my blog: "Granny Grace's crazy stories".

3. My weekend

Write six sentences about your last weekend in your exercise book.

***Examples:* On Friday afternoon I visited my aunt. On Friday night my parents ...**

The simple present and the present progressive in contrast

*

1. You always win!
Kreise die richtigen Formen des *simple present* ein.

Examples: ***Do / Does your mum play football?***
My mum play / plays tennis.

a. Does / Do you like my shoes?

b. Oh no! Not again! Santa never brings / bring me presents!

c. It's not fair! You always wins / win!

d. Lisa and Charly don't watch / doesn't watch TV every day.

2. Are you listening to me?
Beantworte die Fragen im *present progressive*. Denke daran, dass du eine Form von „to be" *(am – is – are)* und die *-ing*-Form des Verbs (*playing, dancing* ...) benötigst.

Examples:
Are you playing football at the moment? – Yes, I'm playing football at the moment.
Is your teacher dancing on his desk? – No, he isn't dancing on his desk. He's sleeping. (sleep)

1. Are your parents eating pizza? – No, ______________________.
______________________. (drink tea)
2. Are we sitting in the classroom? – Yes, ______________________.
3. Is your sister making a mess? – Yes, ______________________.
4. Am I looking terrible in this shirt? – No, ______________________.
______________________. (look nice)

3. Donald's nice day
Schreibe in deinem Heft auf, was Donald normalerweise macht und was er nur heute macht.

Example: ***Donald usually drinks (usually – drink) Lindsay's milk.***
Today he's drinking (drink) some water.

a. Donald (often – sleep) in Lisa's bed. Today he (sleep) in his cage.
b. Donald (sometimes – eat) Bill's chocolate. Today he (eat) a carrot.
c. Donald (usually – watch) horror movies on TV. Today he (read) the newspaper.
d. Donald (often – make) a mess. Today he (wash) his hamster hut.

The simple present and the present progressive in contrast

1. You always win!
Fill in the correct forms in the simple present.

Example: ***Does your mum play football? – No, she doesn't. She plays tennis. (play)***

a. ______________________ you ______________________ my shoes? (like)

b. Oh no! Not again! Santa never ______________________ me presents! (bring)

c. It's not fair! You always ______________________! (win)

d. Lisa and Charly ______________________ TV every day. (not/watch)

2. Are you listening to me?
Complete the questions with the correct form of 'to be' and the *-ing* form of the verb. Then answer the questions.

Examples:
Are you playing football at the moment? (play) – Yes, I'm playing football at the moment.
Is your teacher dancing on his desk? (dance) – No, he isn't dancing on his desk. He's sleeping. (sleep)

1. ______ your parents ________ pizza? (eat) – No, ______________________________.
   ______________________________. (drink tea)
2. ______ we ________ in the classroom? (sit) – Yes, ______________________________.
3. ______ your sister ________ a mess? (make) – Yes, ______________________________.
4. ______ I ________ terrible in this shirt? (look) – No, ______________________________.
   ______________________________. (look nice)

3. Donald's nice day
Write in your exercise book what Donald usually does and what he's doing today.

Example: ***Donald <u>usually drinks</u> (usually/drink) Lindsay's milk. Today he<u>'s drinking</u> (drink) some water.***

a. Donald (often – sleep) in Lisa's bed. Today he (sleep) in his cage.
b. Donald (sometimes – eat) Bill's chocolate. Today he (eat) a carrot.
c. Donald (usually – watch) horror movies on TV. Today he (read) the newspaper.
d. Donald (often – make) a mess. Today he (wash) his hamster hut.
e. Donald (sometimes – play) his drums. Today he (play) the piano.

The simple present and the present progressive in contrast

1. You always win!
Fill in the correct forms in the simple present.

Example: ***Does your mum play football? – No, she doesn't. She plays tennis. (play)***

a. ______________ you ______________ my shoes? (like)

b. Oh no! Not again! Santa never ______________ me presents! (bring)

c. It's not fair! You always ______________! (win)

d. Lisa and Charly ______________ TV every day. (not / watch)

e. ______________ Alex on the bus every morning? – Yes, he usually ______________. (be)

f. ______________ your classmates ______________ maths? – No, they ______________.

They ______________ PE. (love)

2. Are you listening to me?

a. Complete the questions with the correct form of 'to be' and the *-ing* form of the verb. Then answer the questions.

b. Think of one more question and answer in the present progressive. Write it down in 5.

Example: ***Is your teacher dancing on his desk? (dance) – No, he isn't dancing on his desk. He's sleeping. (sleep)***

1. ______ your parents ________ pizza? (eat) – No, ______________________________.
______________________________. (drink tea)

2. ______ we ________ in the classroom? (sit) – Yes, ______________________________.

3. _____ your sister _______ a mess? (make) – Yes, ______________________________.

4. _____ I _______ terrible in this shirt? (look) – No, ______________________________.
______________________________. (look nice)

5. ______________________________? – ______________________________
____

3. Donald's nice day
Write in your exercise book what Donald usually does and think of something that he's doing today. The box helps you.

Example: ***Donald usually drinks (usually / drink) Lindsay's milk. Today he's drinking (drink) some water.***

a. Donald (often – sleep) in Lisa's bed. Today he ...
b. Donald (sometimes – eat) Bill's chocolate. Today he ...
c. Donald (usually – watch) horror movies on TV. Today he ...
d. Donald (often – make) a mess. Today he ...
e. Donald (sometimes – play) his drums. Today he ...

read newspaper
sleep in cage
play piano
wash hamster hut
eat carrot

Lösungen

To be – positive and negative statements

1. *, ** und *** a. is, b. am, c. is, d. are, e. are, f. are, g. am, h. are

2. * a. isn't – is, b. aren't – are, c. aren't – are, d. 'm not – I am

2. ** a. ... isn't a horse. Lindsay is ..., b. ... aren't stupid. Lisa and Charly are ..., c. aren't from New York. You are ..., d. ...'m not a student. I am ...

2. *** a. is ... isn't a horse. Lindsay is ..., b. are ... aren't stupid. Lisa and Charly are ..., c. 'm ... aren't from New York. You are ..., d. are ...'m not a student. I am ...

3. *, ** und *** Individuelle Lösung

To be (short forms) and personal pronouns

1. *, ** und *** a. It, b. you, c. We, d. I, e. He, f. They ** und *** g. you, h. She

2. *, ** und *** a. It's a nice day. b. I'm from Germany. c. They're from London. d. We're in the classroom.

3. *, ** und *** b. They're, c. She's, d. It's, e. You're / It's, f. We're ** und *** g. It's, h. You're *** i. He's, j. It's

4. *, ** und *** Individuelle Lösung

To be – questions

1. * a. 3, b. 1, c. 4, d. 2

1a. ** und *** a. Is, b. Are, c. Are, d. am

1b. ** a. 3, b. 1, c. 4, d. 2

1b. *** a. 3 is, b. 1 aren't, c. 4 aren't, d. 2 are

2. * a. Is your mother from Berlin?, b. Is blue your favourite colour?, c. Are elephants pink?, d. Am I pretty?, e. Is your schoolbag green?

2. ** und *** a. Is your mother from Berlin? – Yes, she is., b. Is blue your favourite colour? – No, it isn't., c. Are elephants pink? – No, they aren't., d. Am I pretty? – Yes, you are. (Bei *** auch möglich Are you pretty? Yes, I am.) , e. Is your schoolbag green? – No, it isn't.

3a. *, ** und *** b. 4, c. 5, d. 3, e. 1

3b. *, ** und *** Individuelle Lösung

3c. *** Individuelle Lösung

Can

1. * a. can't, b. can, c. can't, d. can, e. can

1. ** und *** a. can't read, b. can play, c. can't see, d. can cook, e. can play *** f. can ride

2. * a. Yes, I can. / No, I can't., b. Yes, she can. / No, she can't., c. Yes, she / he can. / No, she / he can't., d. Yes, he can. / No, he can't.

2. ** und *** a. Can you sing? – Yes, I can. / No, I can't., b. Can your mother play tennis? – Yes, she can. / No, she can't., c. Can your friend climb a tree? – Yes, she / he can. / No, she / he can't., d. Can your father cook spaghetti? – Yes, he can. / No, he can't. *** e. Can your music teacher play the piano? – Yes, she / he can. / No, she / he can't.

3. * a. Can birds fly?, b. Can we / you watch TV now?, c. Can we / I go home?, d. Can they buy a new car?

3. ** und *** a. Can birds fly? – can fly, b. Can we / you watch TV now? – can't watch TV, c. Can we / I go home? – can go, d. Can they buy a new car? – can't buy *** e. Can your sister jump high? – can jump

4. *, ** und *** Individuelle Lösung

Have got

1. ** und *** P1: We have got a bike. *, ** und *** P2: It has got a fish. P3: I have got a ball. P4: You have got a book. P5: They have got a laptop.

2. *, ** und *** P2: hasn't got a bike, a ball, a book or a laptop. P3: haven't got a bike, a fish, a book or a laptop. P4: You haven't got a bike, a fish, a ball or a laptop. P5: They haven't a bike, a fish, a ball or a book.

3. *, ** und *** a. Has Charly got … – No, he hasn't. b. Have you got … – Yes, I have. c. Have Lisa and Charly got … – Yes, they have. d. … have you got … – No, we haven't.

4. *, ** und *** Individuelle Lösung

The s-genitive and the possessive determiners

1. *, ** und *** a. teacher's, b. Charly's, c. Lisa and Charly's, d. The kids', e. My sister's, f. The Johnsons' ** und *** g. Bill's – Thomas', h. Superman's *** i. The Webbers', j. The students'

2. *, ** und *** a. my, b. your, c. their, d. her, e. his, f. our, g. your, h. his *(Hat das Tier einen Namen, wird meistens „her / his“ statt „its“ verwendet.)*

3. *, ** und *** a. No, her bed isn't small. b. Yes, his phone is new. c. No, their garden isn't nice. d. Yes, its head is big. e. No, her / his hair isn't grey. ** und *** f. Yes, my / our classroom is pretty. g. No, their bikes aren't cool.

4. *, ** und *** Individuelle Lösung

The simple present – positive statements

1. *, ** und *** gets up – likes – eats – goes – love – says – sits – smiles – talk – say – asks – thinks ** und *** says – listen – are – 'm / am *** laughs – says – think

2. * und ** a. You drink coffee every Sunday. b. Charly plays football every week. c. Lisa / Alex meets Alex / Lisa every morning. *(Die Zeitangaben könnten auch am Satzanfang stehen.)*

2. *** a. I kiss my horse every day. b. You drink coffee every Sunday. c. Charly plays football every week. d. Lisa / Alex meets Alex / Lisa every morning. e. Michelle reads the newspaper every afternoon. *(Die Zeitangaben könnten auch am Satzanfang stehen.)*

3. *, ** und *** Individuelle Lösung

The simple present – negative statements

1. *, ** und *** a. don't like, b. don't play, c. Don't watch, d. doesn't go, e. don't play *** f. don't sleep

2. *, ** und *** a. Rabbits don't eat steak. They eat carrots. b. I don't drink beer every morning. I drink coffee. c. You don't love chocolate for breakfast. You love sandwiches. d. We don't go ice skating in summer. We go ice skating in winter. e. Alex doesn't read a book every night. He watches TV.
3. *, ** und *** Individuelle Lösung

The simple present – questions with 'do'

1. *, ** a. Do, b. do, c. Do, d. Does
1. *** a. Do – don't, b. do – do, c. Do – don't, d. Does – does, e. does – does
2. *, ** und *** a. Does your father play a musical instrument? – Yes, he does. b. Do you live in a flat? – No, I don't. c. Does your grandfather do sport? – No, he doesn't. d. Does your mother eat a lot of sweets? Yes, she does. ** und *** e. Do you help your mum in the kitchen? – No, I don't.
3. *, ** und *** Individuelle Lösung

The simple present – questions with question words

1. * **How?**: Great! By bike. **When?**: At ten o'clock. **Where?**: In London. At school. **Who?**: My friend Kim. My teacher. **Why?**: Because he's from England. Because she's nice.
1. ** **How?**: Great! By bike. Ten years old. **When?**: At ten o'clock. Last week. **Where?**: In London. At school. **Who?**: My friend Kim. My teacher. **Why?**: Because he's from England. Because she's nice. **What?**: Horses. Pizza.
1. *** **How?**: Great! By bike. Ten years old. Sunny and warm. **When?**: At ten o'clock. Last week. **Where?**: In London. At school. In Spain. **Who?**: My friend Kim. My teacher. My mum. **Why?**: Because he's from England. Because she's nice. **What?**: Horses. Pizza.
2. *, ** und *** a. Where, b. When, c. How, d. Who ** und *** e. Why, f. What *** g. How, h. What
3. *, ** und *** a. Where does Mr. Marty live? b. How does Charly get to school? c. What does your brother do on Sundays? *** d. Why do you play basketball?
4. *, ** und *** Individuelle Lösung

Adverbs of frequency

1. *, ** und *** a. I always do my homework at the weekend. b. Bill often waters the flowers at night. c. Lisa and Charly usually get up late on Sundays. d. We sometimes go to church on Christmas. e. You never help me with the cooking.

2a. *** Lindsay never washes the car. *, ** und *** Lindsay often watches TV. Lindsay is always nice. Lindsay usually sleeps on the sofa. ** und *** Lindsay sometimes drinks milk.

2b. *, ** und *** Individuelle Lösung

2c. *** Individuelle Lösung

3. *, ** und *** Individuelle Lösung

Lösungen

Object pronouns

1. * a. Mr. Marty, can you help me? – 4, b. I have to clean it. – 2, c. I love her. – 1, d. Can you make us a sandwich, please? – 5, e. I hate them. – 3

1a. ** und *** a. 4, b. 2, c. 1, d. 5, e. 3

1b. ** und *** a. me, b. it, c. her, d. us, e. them

2. * a. them, b. me, c. you, d. him, e. you, f. her

2. ** und *** a. the answers – them, b. I – me, c. students – you, d. Bill – him, e. Lindsay – you, f. Michelle – her

3. *, ** und *** a. Donuts are great. I love them. b. Hey Santa Claus, can you bring me many presents, please? c. Oh no! the car is broken. Can you repair it, Mr. Webber? d. Ssshhh! Mr Marty wants to tell us something. Please listen to him. / Listen to him, please. *** e. Lisa is mad at you. Talk to her, Charly.

Quantifiers: some and any

1. *, ** und *** a. any, b. some, c. some, d. any ** und *** e. any, f. any – some *** g. any, h. some

2. *, ** und *** Lisa hasn't got any dresses. Lisa has got some chocolate. Lisa hasn't got any sweets. Lisa hasn't got any money. Lisa has got some magazines. Lisa has got some T-shirts. ** und *** Lisa has got some board games. Lisa hasn't got any concert tickets. Lisa hasn't got any books. *** Lisa has got some caps. Lisa has got some pens. Lisa hasn't got any make-up.

3. *, ** und *** Individuelle Lösung

Quantifiers: much and many

1. *, ** und ***

Lisa: … – it's too **much** work. I'm hungry. Can I have something to eat?
Michelle: Mmmmhh, we haven't got **much** food here.
Lisa: Oh, no! Let's write a shopping list.
Michelle: I'm sorry. I haven't got **much** time. Can you do it?
Lisa: OK. How **many** apples are there?
Michelle: There's one old apple.
Lisa: How **much** chocolate do we need?
Michelle: We don't need chocolate, but we haven't got **much** milk in the fridge.
Lisa: All right … so we need milk and apples. That's not **much**.
Michelle: Write down butter, bread, watermelons …
Lisa: How **many** watermelons?
Michelle: Two watermelons, please. ** und *** Oh, and there isn't **much** cat food. Write that down too.
Lisa: OK. Come on! Let's go! Shopping is so **much** fun.
*** Michelle: Well … I think shopping food isn't **much** fun at all. There are too **many** people and too **much** noise.

2. *, ** und *** 1. There isn't much water. 2. There aren't many muffins. 3. There aren't many biscuits. 4. There isn't much sugar. 5. There aren't many strawberries. ** und *** 6. There isn't much cheese. 7. There aren't many carrots.

3. *, ** und *** Individuelle Lösung

The present progressive – positive and negative statements

1. *** It's 9 o'clock on a Saturday and the Webbers **are sitting** in the kitchen.

   *, ** und *** Bill **is reading** the newspaper. Lisa **is doing** something on her phone. Michelle says, "Where's Charly?" No answer ..."Hello? Listen to me, please. Where's Charly?" she shouts. Lisa says, "Sorry, Mum. I**'m / am texting** with Alex. Charly and Lindsay are upstairs. They**'re / are looking** for the mouse." Bill screams "What? I can't believe a mouse **is living** in my house. I hate mice!" Then Charly and Lindsay come into the kitchen. Lindsay **is carrying** something grey in her mouth. "Ugghhh!" Bill shouts and jumps on the table. "Relax, Dad. It's just a toy mouse," Charly says. Michelle and Lisa **are laughing** out loud.

   *** "That's not funny!" Bill shouts. "Relax, Sweetheart. It think, it's funny. Ehhh ... What **is** Donald **doing** there?" says Michelle. "He**'s / is eating** your favourite chocolate, Mum," Lisa answers. "Oh, no!!" Michelle screams. Bill smiles and says "Relax, Sweetheart. I think, it's funny."
2. *, ** und *** b. I'm watching TV. c. Bill is reading a nice book. d. We're playing a board game. e. Cat Lindsay is drinking some milk. ** und *** f. Two mice are eating cheese. *** g. You 're / are drinking (too much) beer.
3. *, ** und *** a. Alex isn't flirting with hamster Donald. He's flirting with Lisa. b. Our grandparents aren't sleeping. They're playing on the PC. c. I'm not drinking a beer. I'm drinking a cup of tea. d. You aren't dancing. You're singing. *** e. We aren't eating hamsters. We're eating frogs. f. Lindsay isn't sleeping on the sofa. She's sleeping in Lisa's bed.

The present progressive – questions

1. *, ** und *** a. Is Lindsay sleeping ... – isn't sleeping, b. Am I looking ... – are looking, c. Are the kids watching ... are watching *** d. Are we having – aren't having – 're having
2. *, ** und *** a. What is Charly watching? b. Who is singing Jingle Bells? c. How is Michelle making her muffins? d. Why is Lisa crying? e. Where are the Johnsons going on holiday?
3. *, ** und *** Individuelle Lösung

The simple past – was / were

1. ** und *** Charly: My day **wasn't** very exciting. Where's mum? *, ** und *** **Was** she here today?

   Bill: No, she **wasn't** here. There **was** a concert at Hyde Park. She and Lisa **were** at this concert.

   Charly: Oh really? What kind of concert **was** that? Heavy metal?

   Bill: No, it **wasn't** heavy metal. What **was** the name of that little singer again? I can't remember. Oh, now I know! Justin Weeper!

   Michelle and Lisa are coming home.

   Lisa: This **was** the best day of my life. Justin **was** so cool and good-looking. And the music **wasn't** just good – it **was** fantastic!

   Michelle: I think the music **wasn't** fantastic at all. Actually it **was** terrible. And there **were** so many fans.

** und *** Charly: What about Alex? Isn't he your boyfriend, Lisa?

Lisa: Alex **was** my boyfriend. It's over. I want Justin now.

*** Bill: Oh dear. When I **was** young, there **were** some nice singers too.

Lisa: Yeah, right. 100 years ago, everything **was** great.

2. *, ** und *** a. Were there any nice boys at the party? – No, there weren't. b. Was your grandfather at the football match yesterday? – Yes, he was. c. Were your parents in the garden last weekend? – No, they weren't. d. Where were you last week? – Last week I was in Spain. e. How was the weather in Spain? – It was terrible: Rainy and cold!
3. *, ** und *** Individuelle Lösung

The simple past (regular verbs) – positive statements

1. *, ** und *** On Tuesday Charly played football. On Wednesday Charly talked to his friends. On Thursday Charly waited for the bus. On Friday Charly watched TV. ** und *** On Saturday Charly washed the car.
2. *, ** und *** When I was a young girl, I **walked** one hour to school every morning – even if it **rained** or **snowed**. At school we **listened** to the teacher all the time. We never **chatted** or **laughed** in the lesson. After school we **hurried** home because there was a lot of work to do. I always **helped** my mum in the kitchen. I **washed** the dishes and **tidied** the kitchen. When all the work was **finished**, my father **played** the piano and we **danced**. We never **watched** TV or **looked** at smartphones.

   ** und *** We **talked** a lot. We really **loved** our family nights.

   *** Last year I **started** my blog: "Granny Grace's crazy stories".
3. *, ** und *** Individuelle Lösung

The simple present and the present progressive in contrast

1. * a. Do, b. brings, c. win d. don't watch
1. ** und *** a. Do – like, b. brings, c. win d. don't watch *** e. Is – is, f. Do – love – don't – love
2. * 1. No, they aren't eating pizza. They are drinking tea. 2. Yes, we're sitting in the classroom. 3. Yes, she's making a mess. 4. No, you aren't looking terrible. You're looking nice.
2. ** und *** 1. Are your parents eating pizza? – No, they aren't eating pizza. They are drinking tea. 2. Are we sitting in the classroom? – Yes, we're sitting in the classroom. 3. Is your sister making a mess? – Yes, she's making a mess. 4. Am I looking terrible in this shirt? – No, you aren't looking terrible. You're looking nice. *** 5. Individuelle Lösung
3. *, ** und *** a. Donald often sleeps in Lisa's bed. Today he's sleeping in his cage. b. Donald sometimes eats Bill's chocolate. Today he's eating a carrot. c. Donald usually watches horror movies on TV. Today he's reading the newspaper./Today he's washing his hamster hut. d. Donald often makes a mess. Today he's washing his hamster hut./Todays he's reading the newspaper ** und *** e. Donald sometimes plays his drums. Today he's playing the piano.